Elisha Benjamin Andrews

Wealth and Moral Law

Elisha Benjamin Andrews

Wealth and Moral Law

ISBN/EAN: 9783744667029

Printed in Europe, USA, Canada, Australia, Japan

Cover: Foto ©Suzi / pixelio.de

More available books at **www.hansebooks.com**

Wealth and Moral Law

WEALTH AND MORAL LAW

THE CAREW LECTURES

FOR 1894

HARTFORD THEOLOGICAL SEMINARY

BY

E. BENJAMIN ANDREWS, D.D., LL.D.

President of Brown University

HARTFORD, CONN.
Hartford Seminary Press
1894

Press of The Case, Lockwood & Brainard Co.

PREFATORY NOTE

The original purpose of these lectures is sufficiently indicated in the opening paragraphs of Lecture I. Since their delivery, it has been thought that they may with advantage be made accessible to a wider public.

The industrial life of our time creates many new moral problems, some of which are ever coming home to every man's business and bosom. Multitudes of good people, unable to solve these, find them a source of incessant mental distress. Most of us do not wish to engage in practices which are wrong, or to countenance such. On the other hand we are anxious not to condemn deeds or policies that are good and right. Men need more instruction in the concrete particulars of duty, more light upon the often hardly visible distinction between right and wrong in social and economic conduct. The ethical teaching of schools and colleges must, from the nature of the case, be mainly theoretical and general, and it therefore very imperfectly supplies this want even for liberally educated persons. Neither the secular nor the religious press canvasses the finer questions of Applied Ethics with much delicacy or depth. Even the pulpit has not in recent years duly discharged this part of its high office. Indeed, I fear that, since the Reformation, at any rate, the pulpit has at no time done this. Happily, one sees signs that preachers are determined to be more faithful here.

It is hoped that this book will, so far as it goes, do something to meet the want referred to, affording safe and valuable guidance touching the important difficulties in conduct which it discusses.

Though the Lectures seek to approach their subjects from the popular side, the treatment will, it is believed, be found sufficiently scientific to interest general and even critical students of economics.

The range of topics is limited, and each is so vast and complex that much which should be said upon each is necessarily omitted. The volume is therefore far from being a complete manual of Practical Ethics. It indicates, however, how much a treatise of that nature is needed, and may perhaps be considered as offering some hints upon the course and the method which such might well follow.

Phases of subjects presented in these pages the author has more fully expounded in various reviews and critical publications. For convenience, the following are named: "Journal of Social Science" for 1889 and 1890; "Quarterly Journal of Economics," Jan., 1889; "Yale Review," May, 1893; "North American Review," Nov., 1892; "International Journal of Ethics," April, 1892; "The New World," June, 1892; "Journal of Political Economy" [Chicago], Dec., 1892.

THE AUTHOR

Brown University,
    May Day, 1894.

CONTENTS

Lecture I
General View of Wealth in its Moral Relations, . . 9

Lecture II
Trusts and other Combinations of Capital, . . - 30

Lecture III
Economic Evils as Aided by Legislation, . 50

Lecture IV
Economic Evils Due to Social Conditions, . . - 69

Lecture V
Socialism, ... 91

Lecture VI
Weal and Character, ... - 114

I
WEALTH IN ITS MORAL RELATIONS
GENERAL VIEW

THESE LECTURES are meant to expound a few of those economic truths which bear the most vital relation to the work of the Christian ministry. Little of what I say will be directly preachable, but all of it, I hope, will help us to preach wisely upon certain delicate matters which efficient pulpit ministration cannot help touching. If it was ever possible to set forth a full gospel without canvassing rights and wrongs connected with wealth, poverty, legislation, and social order, it is so no longer. Equally impossible is it to say, on many of these themes, what one ought, unless one is more or less acquainted with economic principles. But the good minister is much more than a preacher. He is a leader, adviser, administrator. Many consciences he almost alone informs. Like his Master, he has continually to do with the poor. He either himself collects and disburses charity funds or else directs this work. His words, attitudes, and temper touching economic things sway for good or for ill those of multitudes who never see or hear him. From every point of view it is important that he should know what he is saying when he broaches an economic topic.

He will thus be not the less a minister, but more so.

Political Economy is not the Gospel, but it may be made nobly ancillary thereto. Still is it the minister's work, a higher than which no mortal can have, to turn men from sin and death to righteousness and life. Let none of us be led by the great sociological zeal and revelations of our age to think less highly of the ministerial calling. Social Science by itself will save no man. The command, Preach the Word, is as valid, imperative, and important as ever. Only we want wisdom to preach it roundly and well.

This first lecture treats the relation of wealth to the moral law in a quite general way, reserving some more special phases of the subject for later remark. Ought wealth to exist at all, and, if so, how should it be owned and how should it be used?

I proceed to lay down several propositions:

I. The existence of wealth is morally legitimate.

Whatever is needful to the life and weal of men has a right to be. Wealth is certainly such. Perhaps wealthy men are not necessary. Very likely wealth so congested as it often is now is undesirable. Possibly communal wealth would be preferable to wealth individually owned. But wealth, at some rate, on some tenure, men must have or die.

Obvious as this truth is, it has been denied. Theorists have declared that the world could get on as well without wealth as with, and perhaps even better. It must be that utterances of this sort confuse wealth with particular manifestations or tenures of it. Wealth is simply humanity's stock in trade, its tools and machinery wherewith to get its living. Everyone must recognize that without a vast supply of such instrumentalities the very existence of our race in its present extent would be impossible. Comfort, culture, civilization would be still further out of the question. So long as all must use each moment of time and ounce of strength in fighting hunger, savagery is the inevitable lot. Most people little consider how completely the high and precious interests of men, including the spread of the Gospel and the happiness of the poor themselves, depend upon the creation and the piling together of goods and chattels. Lucre is lucre, nothing more. It will save no man's soul. But it is, after all, a quite indispensable thing.

II. Wealth is necessary not as an evil but as a good.

Confessedly, wealth is often hoarded with an evil intent, and often put to wrong uses; but it is blasphemy to stigmatize it as an evil on this account. Any blessings of God, even life itself, can be misused and turned into curses; but this is their misfortune, not their fault.

If the charge against wealth as an evil means aught more than that evils accompany it, it is false. No one calls machinery an evil because of its friction, although, so far as man's present knowledge extends, the friction is inevitable. The ills attending wealth are much more likely than those of machinery to be some day eliminated. It is certain baneful circumstances of wealth, not its substance, which deserves hard words. Some of these vicious circumstances we shall canvass later.

III. The wealth, however large, of one man does not necessarily involve the poverty of any other man.

It is a great error to suppose that the wealth of the world, or of any community, is a fixed, limited sum, like the shares in a bank, so that if you should get a dollar more than you now have, I must put up with a dollar less than I now have. There are indeed cases where one's gain involves another's loss: where, that is, a man's gain is gotten through open or occult, legal or illegal robbery. But wealth can increase, increase to any sum, without this or any injustice. The wealth of any land or neighborhood is like leavened dough, not like a definite sum. Divide and subdivide, and each mass, if rightly used, speedily becomes as great as the whole was. Every day, in the market, or wherever men traffic, you may convince yourself that the inevitable tendency of natural trade is to enrich all the parties to it. The difference between business and gambling is simply this, that in gambling one party or the other must lose, while in business both may gain, and commonly do. There is point and truth to it when we speak of "making" money and property. A swindler or a thief may "get" money, his victim being just so much the poorer for it; but a true man of business "makes" money, no one being the poorer in consequence, but everyone the richer. He literally increases the total stock of property on the earth. And that, whether or not any of his pelf ever falls to you or me personally, is to the community at large a palpable benefit.

IV. Whatever may be sometimes the case, as things are, it is no sin to get rich or to be rich.

This is not the same as saying that wealth is legitimate, because vast wealth might be present without a single rich man — precisely what socialists wish and expect. Should their *régime* ever be launched and work as they predict, private riches would be wrong. But, prevailing our present individualistic system, which, mark, no one and no group of us can change at will, the private massing and holding of wealth not only does not necessarily involve aught of injury to anyone, but may, and probably in most cases does, benefit all concerned.

No doubt a man may accumulate money in a sinful spirit, or, may accumulate *bona fide* yet in such ways as to harm his fellows. Those already rich, it is likely, often sin by withholding more than is meet. Very few people of means are in danger of being too generous. Still, the gaining or the possession of wealth, unless made an end, need not be a sin. Nay, a man's very best way to please God and carry out the law of love may possibly be to make himself as rich as he can become. The command of God declares against the selfish gathering and holding of money, but never condemns one simply for possessing money, however much. It only forbids you to be a miser, enjoining you in Christ's name to get and use money, as we are bound to do all things, for the weal of our fellowmen. Whosoever piles higher the world's stock of capital, "makes" money, that is, instead of taking riches which some one else has created, is a public benefactor. His thrift and gain are gifts from God, not at your expense or mine, but to the profit of both and of all. If wealth comes to any man as fruit of his honest deal or toil, let him thank God for it without reserve, in full confidence that, so far from his good fortune involving his neighbor's loss, God has blessed all the rest of us in blessing him.

V. Important as are the distribution and the tenure of wealth, the existence or supply of it is more important.

Doubtless it makes some difference whether the bulk of a people's wealth is owned privately or by the state, and whether, if privately owned, it is well scattered about or badly congested. For all this, the great thing is to have the wealth in existence. If wealth is there, it is certain to get itself used, in the main, for a more or less general good. Wealth can indeed be wasted out and out, doing good to no one; and this is equally possible, as it is equally unfortunate, under any tenure. But no rational motive prompts to such pure, purposeless waste of wealth. What does occur to a lamentable extreme is the selfish use of wealth for private instead of general good. It is the spectacle of such prodigality, when so many are poor all about us, which is causing the wide conviction in our time that private ownership of land and capital ought to be done away. Such vain dissipation of wealth is a dire evil, which, very possibly, a system of socialism or the public ownership of productive wealth might assuage. But I beg attention to the fact that, though tenure be private as now, and many fortunes great, rich men's selfishness itself forces them to divide their goods, to a great extent, with others. No man can enjoy his wealth save by using it, and to use it, even in the most selfish and sinful way, he must employ labor, in part directly by hiring it himself, and in part indirectly by the purchase of goods.

It is, indeed, desirable that wealth be well distributed. It is important to have it all used, none of it wasted, all used to promote the general good, none of it to afford mere private satisfaction. But what is of most consequence after all is that wealth should be; for, if it exists in sufficient amplitude, however shackled and misapplied, the poorest of us must get some benefit from it.

VI. For the present, millionaires, however dangerous, are desirable.

Few thoughtful people hesitate to admit that a certain danger, perhaps very great, attaches to the colossal massing of wealth with which our day is familiar. The advantages of wealth would probably be greater and the disadvantages less if it could be pretty well parcelled out. The ideal society would be one which produced few monstrously rich people, and forced none really to be poor. Then, if any were distressingly poor, the fault would clearly be their own. I frankly avow my belief, or at least my hope, that the trend of things is in the direction of such relative equality in temporal fortune, toward a social condition where many of the immense and indispensable undertakings for which we now have to rely on massed capital will be assumed by the state. I hope for the time when the poorest people will have possessions enough to give them genuine sympathy with those of still greater resources and influence. For such a benign change let all Christians ever work and pray! Absolute equality among men, who desires? But every lover of his race must desiderate a social state admitting such relative equality in human conditions as shall make universal fellow-feeling a possibility.

However, it is certain that no such earthly millenium is possible without a pretty radical reorganization of human society, a reorganization which cannot be brought about on simple notification, and for the tardy coming of which wealthy people are no more responsible than others. Meantime, while we thus wait, in spite of ourselves, in spite alike of the rich and of the poor, for that beatific leveling up, and that leveling down — for it must be this, too, in large degree — of the distinctions in fortune which now prevail, it is at once inevitable and indispensable that great fortunes should exist. It is inevitable, because thrift and business ability pile up these fortunes, as we see on every hand. It is indispensable, because the great undertakings which advanced civilization calls for, cannot be carried through without the employment of capital in vast masses, far beyond the resources of people just ordinarily well off. Nor can such enterprises be accomplished legitimately, or even possibly, by capital that is borrowed in small sums, as they involve too much risk.

It is true that any required amounts could be gotten together from the savings of people not rich, consisting, that is, of ordinary banking capital. But no honest man would think of employing such capital in enterprises involving great risk like those which have given recent civilization its peculiar splendor, as initiating telegraphy, steam and electric traction and propulsion, physical and chemical experimentation, opening mines, and so on. Dishonest men would use banking or any capital in such projects if they could get it, but they could not get it. Such immense works, invaluable for human advancement, always have been carried through, and in the nature of the case must still be, by men who have vast funds in their own right, of which, therefore, they can, unhindered, risk the loss.

We will hasten forward to a better distribution of wealth just as fast as evolution will carry us, but meantime let us not scruple to admit the advantages, along with the disadvantages, if you please, of these mountains of wealth in private hands over which so many complain. Grant that society is less well off than it would be if the more even distribution had come; it is yet certain that society is infinitely better off than it would be during the delay of that better time, were those great heaps of wealth away.

VII. Giving in charity may be overdone.

One often hears it said that wealth is good only to do good with, that is, to give away in benevolence. Vastly desirable as it may be that great amounts of money should be given away in charity, it must still be laid down as the rule that on the whole the best way to do good to our fellows by means of our wealth is to use our wealth in employing our fellows; that is, to invest our resources as capital, so as to support honest, industrious men and women in earning wages. When rich people take from their spending money, their luxury money, which they would not in any event use in business, to effect expenditures in the line of charity, if only the objects of charity are rightly chosen, good is done; but when a rich man takes money from a bank or withholds money from his business in order to use the same in charity, he is at best doing good in one direction at the expense of good in another. He is lowering the rate of wages, or perhaps making it impossible for certain honest people who would gladly work, to earn any wages at all. Such cases are of frequent occurrence.

Even when the effect of charity would be thus deleterious in one way, the charity may notwithstanding be desirable on the whole. In such cases, after all the conditions are studied, we are to take the course which seems likely to produce the largest net good. Yet certainly there are many instances where rich people, being solicited to give, actually accomplish more good by keeping their money invested in business than they could secure by the desired benevolence. Were not the greater part of the wealth now existing used productively, soon there would be no wealth to use charitably.

VIII. Giving in charity may be wrongly done.

As Stanton Coit says: "While we are striving to avoid the worst possible calamity, which is hunger with enforced idleness, we must also strive to avoid the next worst calamity, which is enforced idleness with plenty to eat. In the testimony of men who become criminals we find that the first six weeks out of work is a period of torture. Men rise at break of day. They walk the streets night and day in search of work. The second six weeks they lose all energy. The third six weeks they say, 'We never cared to work.' Men who are long in idleness not only lose their skill; they lose their manliness, their independence."*

To such we can be truly charitable only by finding them work. Usually food and clothing ought to be given to none but the sick and incapable. The things to do for other destitutes is to find or furnish them

---

* Carnegie Hall Address, N. Y. City, Dec. 24, 1893. Pres. Gilman, in the *Christian Union* for Feb. 17, 1894, lays down the excellent principles that: 1. Charity should be carefully organized throughout any community, to prevent duplication of agencies, fraud, and waste of force. 2. Save in emergencies, like fire, accident, or sudden illness, charity should be guided by personal cognizance of the wants to be relieved. Indiscriminate almsgiving is most reprehensible. 3. The best of all charities is not to give something for nothing but to give something in return for industry, labor, economy, self-sacrifice, and self-help.

something to do. And the employment provided must not be disguised charity, but such as will prove of real advantage to the whole community.

Every year or two some earnest philanthropist, seeing the evil of feeding beggars at the door, institutes a wood-yard, where wood can be sawn and split by tramps. In order to make the business possible, the wood has to be sold at a price lower than the one prevailing in the market. What follows? This, that self-sustaining business in the same line is made more difficult by this unnatural and forced competition, so that more or fewer of the honest and hard-working people who have heretofore engaged in it are thrown out of employment. The tramp is thus helped to ruin industrious and frugal men and turn them into paupers. Private persons cannot provide work for unemployed people on any considerable scale without involving such mischief. Only the municipality or the state can do this. Such aid, too, needs to be carefully managed, but it should be boldly tried in times like the present.

In many such cases, it is hard for benevolent individuals to determine what to do. I believe it best, usually at any rate, to support the tramps in idleness rather than use them to rob honest laborers of employment. Such a course may be worse for the tramp's character, but it is likely that this cannot suffer very much anyway, while it is far better for both the character and happiness of those who are still industrious.

Few persons see the baneful working of spurious charity. It involves, among other, two terrific evils.

One of them is economic. Your money, your capital is thrown away, wasted. Think how much that means. It implies not only that you are so much poorer, but that the poorer are so much poorer. You might have put your hundred dollars in the bank. Next day some man proposing to build a factory or a railway, or to start a store or engage in some other useful business giving employment to labor, would have borrowed that money to help put in effect his commendable purpose, thus benefiting the entire community by the assistance which your funds would have given him. Now he cannot do this. The enterprise which he wished to begin will not begin. The laborers whom he wanted to hire remain idle. At least some who, but for your wasteful deed, might to-day have been earning wages, are not earning them, or they might have been earning a certain rate of wages, but you have forced them down to a lower rate. All this to pamper in idleness members of the community most of whom are useless.

But this is not the worst. More deplorable than the fact that certain laborers have been thrown out of employment or docked in wages is the terrific waste of labor force which is brought about by giving to men and women that which they could themselves earn. It is a premium on idleness. It is incredible how soon people who are granted such a disadvantageous advantage will decline in economic spirit. If they can be supported they will little by little become willing to be. The disposition to toil, which is at the basis of all the community's prosperity, is destroyed.

The other fearful evil connected with loose giving is a moral one. The loss of economic character merges insensibly into a loss of moral character. Idleness is the mother of vice. The man who is willing that you should support him if you please, after a time becomes determined that you shall support him whether you please or not. If you will not give, he will take. This is always the tendency. Misinformed, thoughtless, irrational charity is probably responsible for hardly less vice than intemperance itself.

We continually hear tirades against the purchase of clothing from sweaters. Christian people have been enjoined by all means never to trade with the wicked men who screw down their help to starvation wages. The story of the "sweated" victims, the poor women made to work twenty hours out of the twenty-four for a pittance of two shillings a day or less, never breathing pure air or seeing the open sunlight, is indeed a pitiable one. But that desperate estate can never be made better by any agreement to boycott the persons who pay the too scanty wages. The economic condition thus touchingly portrayed is due to deeper causes. If I refuse to buy of sweaters, how, I ask, am I certain that I am not, after all, employing sweaters indirectly? Society can never be sure upon this point without a trustworthy standing committee to supervise the entire business of the dealers said to be guiltless of sweating. Some of these may themselves be mistaken, using starved work-women without knowing it.

But suppose we were somehow able to be quite certain that the wares which we purchased were produced entirely by well-paid labor. What would be the meaning of this? Simply that out of an immense army of poor people ready to work for a starvation wage, a few had been arbitrarily selected to receive more. It would amount to a roundabout way of bestowing charity, by the use of our tailors, dressmakers, etc., as our agents. They of course could not sell to us at the low prices charged by the firms who still continued to "sweat."

Were the well-to-do to take from their luxury-expenditure the extra sums needed to clothe themselves in this benevolent way, some net good would probably be done; but so surely as this plan of benevolence were widened enough to relieve any considerable number of "sweater's" victims, goodly amounts would be withdrawn from the wages-fund of the community to the injury of wage-workers in general. Many of these would then sink into the class that we began by trying to help, requiring larger and larger subventions to keep that class from dropping back to its old wretchedness, with larger and larger subtractions from the wages-fund, and so on over and over.

IX. *Wealthy people's chief sin of omission is idleness.*

The very common mode of speech which sets the rich and the poor over against each other, as if the interests of the two classes were opposite, is misleading in the extreme. The proper distinction lies between the thrifty rich and poor on the one hand, and the thriftless rich and poor on the other. Every man, rich or poor, who works and saves is, so far, the friend of his kind, and every man, rich or poor, who is idle, improvident, or wasteful, is, so far, the foe of his kind. The least understood part of this truth relates to the rich, and this part I wish to emphasize.

No people whatever deserve better of the community, poor included, than the industrious and frugal rich. To class them with the other rich and then decry the vices of the rich, is an outrageous slander as well as a crime against clear thinking. Hardly any among humanity's benefactors deserve heartier or more lasting benedictions from the toiling masses than the great captains of industry, like Thomas Brassey, Ferdinand de Lesseps, Ezra Cornell, and Cornelius Vanderbilt. Never confuse such men, simply because they are rich, with vagabond millionaires, or with the wealthy who have inherited all that they own and never earned a cent. The diligent rich are our friends, the idle rich are our foes. The idle rich have to live. They usually much more than live; they fare sumptuously every day. This means that they are leeches upon the body industrial and suck its blood. That process is little understood, whether by the idle rich themselves or by others.

When a man inherits wealth, what is it that in strict fact takes place? To a little extent, it is likely, he actually takes over some realized wealth; houses, furniture, pictures, plates, horses, and carriages; but it would be strange if such things formed the bulk of his heritage. The greater part is nearly certain to consist in stocks, bonds, and mortgages; that is, signs of the legal right, thus far respected by society, to take and consume year by year certain shares of what industrious people, rich and poor, from year to year produce. The wealth used this year, given away, thrown away by the idle rich, is for the most part less than two years old. They did nothing to create it. Society, following an old custom, permitted them to do what St. Paul forbade, eat though they wrought not.

Probably laws of inheritance ought not to be repealed. Unless men can bequeath something to their children they will lack one incentive to work and save. But two reforms touching this matter are, I imagine, certain to come. Bequests will be made more difficult, through laws of taxation diverting to the public chest large percentages of sums thus bestowed; and, quite as important, a more Christian sentiment will render the use, by wealthy men and women, for their own behoof, of wealth which they have not created, first, disreputable and then disgraceful.

X. Wealthy people's chief sin of commission is waste, in the form of idle luxury.

Mark, I speak of idle luxury, for there is luxury which is not idle. The outlay required for keeping one's body and mind in form and function for the work of life, including necessary relaxation, is not idle luxury. Much of it ought not to be named luxury at all. To use a moderate proportion of one's income in travel, in hearing fine concerts, or to purchase good books or works of art, is not idle luxury, even though the good thus procured is not of the nature of strictly necessary relaxation. The expenditure has contributed to our elevation in the dignity of rational beings. As a rule, such uses of wealth are justifiable in proportion to the elevation of the needs to which they minister and in proportion to the number of human beings who are to participate in the good.

There are, indeed, cases where wealth is consumed in this way, for objects wholly legitimate, as building a church, sending money to the heathen, or investment in fine art for the public behoof, over which, however, one who is determined to follow the moral law must deliberate long. Outlays of such a kind certainly withdraw capital from the support of labor. In proposing an expenditure of this order, he who loves his fellowmen will raise the question whether his capital is likely to effect more good on the whole and in the long run laid out as proposed or laid out productively. More imperative still is that query in case I meditate gratifying a personal need, however noble. So far as this life is concerned, there may be an absolute conflict between my highest interest and that of the laboring class.

Whatever our opinion touching the propriety of these indulgences, luxury in which people invest merely for their own private satisfaction, without any betterment to their characters and without any advantage of any kind either to themselves or to the great world of their fellowmen, is certainly idle, and therefore illicit luxury. Any investment of money which merely gratifies vanity is wrong, and one judging never so charitably must conclude that there are many such outlays. Houses, grounds, equipage and clothing are not seldom provided in amplitude far beyond the owner's utmost need, and with a magnificence and display so defiant of taste that one cannot possibly refer them to aught but vanity. Many such investments are not only idle but positively harmful to those who make them, as when a spendthrift gives an all-night entertainment costing thousands of dollars, which leaves only "withered flowers, rumpled vanities, deranged stomachs, and overtaxed nerves." Anyone who will reflect can easily make himself sick at heart by computing what a large proportion of existing wealth has been put into forms which are a moral as well as a business disadvantage to the owners. Such wealth affords no wages to labor, being lost to society as truly as if sunk in the sea.

There is a very common and stubborn opinion in denial of this, to the effect that all such lavishness, since it commonly involves more or less labor, is an advantage to the poor and not a curse. This notion is purely superficial and erroneous. The expenditures characterized are forms of cruel, unrighteous waste. He who sees through them cannot say one word to justify them. It is true that while the waste is going on laborers may be employed. This fact confuses many, blinding them to the radical difference between these and productive applications of wealth.

Reflect a little. If I have in my vault or storehouse a million gold eagles or twenty million bushels of wheat, and, availing myself of my legal privilege, determine to sink them in the sea, I am powerless to do this without employing more or less labor. Is the waste, therefore, a good? My deed, as giving a little work to those needing it, may of course be dubbed "good" in comparison with what it would have been had I annihilated the property by a breath, but this is the very utmost that can be said in its favor.

The illustration perfectly brings out the evil of all waste. If I erect a house needlessly large or fine, I of course employ labor in so doing, but when it is completed, the capital embodied in it has for ever ceased to do good in that or in any way; whereas, had I used the same sum in a factory that was needed, while it would have done during the erection all the good accomplished in the building of the house, this would have been not the end but only the beginning of that capital's benign career. From that moment it would have been engaged, in conjunction with labor, in the creation of new capital, much if not all of which would have entered into partnership with it in creating still other capital to sustain still other labor, and so on in ceaseless and merciful round. The modern world could not learn a truer, and it could hardly learn a more useful lesson than that all idle luxury is waste and that all waste is a crime against society.

To sum up. We have seen that the existence of wealth is legitimate; that wealth is necessary not as an evil but as a good; that the wealth, however large, of one man, does not necessarily involve the poverty of any other man; that, as things are, it is no sin to get rich or to be rich; that it makes comparatively little difference in whose hands wealth is or to what tenure it is subject provided it exists and is used; that, for the present, millionaires, however dangerous, are desirable; that giving in charity may be overdone; that giving in charity may be wrongly done; that wealthy people's chief sin of omission is idleness; and that wealthy people's chief sin of commission is luxury in the form of senseless waste.

II
TRUSTS AND OTHER COMBINATIONS OF CAPITAL

WARNING was given in the last lecture that the treatment of subjects there was general and that some of the propositions advanced would have to be brought up again, perhaps with slight modifications. Suggestions were offered in that lecture about the high organization of wealth through co-operation; but enough still remains to be said on this to occupy us the present hour.

It requires but little observation to assure one that the competitive system of industry is fast passing away. It is on every hand succumbing to trusts and other combinations for production and distribution. In agriculture, in some simple forms of manufacturing, and in retail trade, competition persists more or less perfectly, and bids fair to do so for a long time to come. But, in almost every line of activity where combination is possible, and it is possible in nearly all, combination of some kind either already prevails or is in process of establishment.

Trade combinations are of various sorts. There are mere monopolies, where certain parties, few or numerous, sufficiently control the entire market to determine the prices at which wares are bought and sold. Then there are cases where different dealers, not closely bound together, have an understanding not to sell under such and such prices. Pools form a third variety of combination. Regular contracts to allow special rates in return for exclusive trade are a fourth. Corners, of the well-known sort, make a fifth. I mention as sixth a form of combination which is usually called a trust, but not very properly so. A small firm sells out to a larger one, receiving a lease in return, and perhaps also some stock. It then goes on in apparent independence, though really under the thumb of the purchasing party. In the trust proper, or unincorporate trust, making a seventh class, several corporations place their stock in the hands of certain trustees, who, issuing trust certificates in return for such stock, so that the profits of the consolidated concern may be properly passed round, yet themselves, owning or at least holding the stock, direct, more or less completely, all that each of the corporations does. This is the trust *par excellence*, made so familiar in the earlier history of the Standard Oil Trust, the Cotton Oil Trust, the Sugar Trust, and the Whiskey Trust. The eighth and last kind of combination is the incorporated trust, an arrangement to which most if not all of the old unincorporated trusts have now been driven in order to avoid the attacks of the law. This change does not alter the form or the purpose of their activity in the slightest. It simply makes them legal.

Although these bandings together of capitalists are

now usually protected by law, I call special attention to the fact that the system of combined business is not originally due to legislation or to any extent kept up thereby. Combination has sprung from the very soul of our old, *laissez-faire*, competitive sort of industry. These monopolies daily arising to new power and numbers, are the logical and inevitable result of that industrial liberty which was formerly our boast. They are the products of economic and social forces, not of statutes.

At the beginning of this century competition was almost universally considered a sort of divinely appointed instrumentality for the fixing of prices in a just manner. If, it was said, given dealers charge more than cost of production plus a living profit, others will undersell them; if less than this is the price, dealers will fail, competition become less severe, and prices recover the fair level.

Men at last saw, however, that competition did not always work in this benign way. If the operation specified was the normal effect in small and simple industries, quite a different result revealed itself in massive and complex production. In this, the manufacturer first in the field might charge for his products far above cost and reasonable profit, and long continue to do so, before capital, ever apt to be timid, would take the risk of competing. When, on the other hand, competition did begin, it was nearly certain to go too far, pushing prices as much below the normal figure as they previously were above, leading to crises and failures, with vast losses, to the immense net depletion of public wealth. From perception of this destructive agency attending competition arose, in the most natural way, the tendency of capitalists to try co-operation and be rid of competition.

Acrimony of competition was not the only force which prompted business rivals to join hands. They were pushed to this also by the fall in prices fatally incident to the vicious monetary system from which the world has been suffering since 1873. While prices are going down all the time, men are loth to enter upon productive industry without some special guaranty of safety and of profit, such as was not necessary in times of rising prices and industrial prosperity. This motive for combination, to gain shelter from industrial heavy weather, like the mere wish to escape competition, takes effect in a perfectly natural and logical manner.

The combine is thus the brother of the protective tariff, and not its child, as so many allege. Most trusts are little affected by tariffs, flourishing about equally whether customs-duties are high or low. Some are entirely independent of tariff legislation. The Cotton Oil Trust is so. Another set would be more or less interfered with by a reduction of the tariff. The Starch Trust is one of these. It was built upon the tariff, and would perish were this support withdrawn. The great Sugar Trust has derived little aid from tariff acts, and would not be crushed by out-and-out free trade. At least two American firms of sugar refiners are strong enough to defy all changes in sugar duties. Were these removed they would at once combine with each other, and, if necessary, with foreign refiners.

The Standard Oil Trust is not in any sense indebted to customs legislation. There is, to be sure, a duty on petroleum, but it as yet has no effect whatever. After a time it will come to mean something. Russian oil is now strongly competing with ours abroad. As this competition waxes severer and presses nearer home, our tariff on oil may certainly come in to help the Standard keep up its prices. If, after that time arrives, the tariff should be thrown off, the Standard would almost certainly ally itself with the Russian producers.

This, I conceive, is going to be the general course of mammoth industry as the world grows smaller. The governmental protection of industries by tariffs will more and more give way to self-protection on their part, through international combinations. The tariff question is ere long to be removed from politics by the irresistible force of events.

Lest some think me mistaken in supposing that competition is vanishing from the business world, I wish to make it clear that monopoly often exists where it does not appear.

Not a few suppose that monopoly is impossible in an industry so long as any sort of competition exists there. If the competition is other than formal, this is of course true; but, in a great number of businesses where what is called competition exists, the competition is not real but simply formal.

People affirm that the Standard Oil Trust, for

instance, cannot be in the enjoyment of a monopoly, because there remain active refineries not leagued with it. The argument is thought to be re-enforced by the observation that the number of outside concerns has increased, perhaps even doubled, since the trust went into effect. A moment's reflection will show the belief to be unwarranted. It is not necessary, in order that a great business may be a monopoly, or, what implies the same, keep a higher than competitive price upon its goods, that it should directly control the entire production. Immediate mastery of a decided majority is practically the mastery of all, and insures to outside dealers as well as to the allies whatever advance of price is realized.

No one will question that the great French Copper Syndicate enormously elevated the price of copper above what competition would have made it, yet it purchased only about three-fifths of the world's entire product. This enabled it to dictate prices to consumers, and all the little producers not in the syndicate came in for a part of the advance. This syndicate, a combination of the very loosest order, lasted nearly eighteen months, and during its continuance imposed upon the commodity in all the markets of the world a purely arbitrary price not far from 100 per cent. above what it would naturally have been.

Every trust or combine known has to encounter formal competition more or less severe. If the total absence of this is required to secure monopoly, there is not a monopoly on earth. The Cotton Oil

Syndicate, the Whiskey Union, the Steel Rail League, and all the rest throughout the lengthy list, are met by a certain species of opposition. They do not mind this, however, for the most of them are as sure of a monopoly with it as without.

Combination in industry is to be permanent. Many cling to the delusion that these mighty combinations of capital are to pass away and the old-time competition to return. Bills have been brought before half the legislatures of the Union to compel free competition by making trade syndicates absolutely illegal. To my mind there is no question that such legislation will be vain. The age of competition as we have known it has gone for ever.* Recall it? As well try to waken the dead. In simple industries, whose capital is small and little specialized, competition has worked well and will continue. The weakest party drops from the strife to-day, to-morrow the next weakest, and so on. But each loss is slight. The unfortunate employer lets himself for wages, and his stock passes to creditors. In such businesses competition is the best practical way to insure a healthy life. Not so when the contestants are industrial Titans, each with a plant worth its millions, much of it so specialized that to relinquish business is

---

* On this see the author's article "Individualism as a Sociological Principle," *Yale Review*, May, 1893. Other thoughts to be touched upon are more fully treated in "The Economic Law of Monopoly," *Journal of Social Science* for 1889, and in "Trusts According to Official Investigation," *Quarterly Journal of Economics*, Jan., 1889.

to sink it utterly. In such cases, which more and more each year represent the world's industry, competition cannot end with a little friction. It grinds, and, in time, kills. The great mill, placed at a disadvantage by position, by some tariff act, or perhaps by railway discrimination, is yet forbidden to shut down. That were to lose all. Better keep running and lose less than all. The least penny over fixed charges and running expenses is better than nothing. Down at least to that dead line the strife is certain to go on, the stockholders impoverishing themselves that their mills may compete. At last a bankrupt sale ensues, machinery going for junk, the building left to collapse from decay. The victors survive, but of course poorer because of the war. Here, too, competition has proved a regulator — as Cæsar kept the peace in Gaul.

Men have learned of a much milder and more successful regulator, — combination. Instead of keeping up that mortal conflict, they unite, pool their interests, make common cause against others trying to enter the field, parcel out the production in as fair a way as possible, and fix buying and selling prices so that all alike may realize gains. No part of the causality involved in this process is of a temporary nature. The history of the Standard and Cotton Oil Trusts make it certain, it seems to me, that a combination of this sort, involving an absolute monopoly which no power on earth can overthrow, may, with proper skill and capital, be set up in almost any substantive industry.

One of the causes mentioned which brought about

the military organization of capital, I mean the long-continued fall in general prices, may of course pass away, though there is too little present prospect of this; but the influence of it has been affecting us long enough to let the world behold how good and how pleasant it is for business brethren to dwell together in unity, and I do not believe that the lesson is ever to be unlearned. Not hap or whim has made combination the industrial fashion of the day, but rigid social laws; nor is there any prospect that these will ever cease to have this effect. Every great industry is destined to take on complete solidarity of organization, and to maintain the same in perpetuity.

These monopolies may work society immeasurable evil. Unless somehow regulated they will certainly so result. The system of combines is not to be held responsible for the doubtful methods and rapacity which some of them have displayed in coming into existence. Rank rebates on freight extorted from railroads, summary methods with competitors, and so on, whether justifiable or not, will not continue. Reasonable foreboding points in a different direction.

I ask the reader specially to note, for it is widely overlooked or denied, that when a business comes under the trust form, no mere economic law is going to force it to deal fairly with society. So far as economic law is concerned, it may, and, unless seriously, systematically looked after, probably will, prove rapacious instead.

When a commodity is produced under trust conditions, cost does not regulate selling prices. This is done quite arbitrarily for a time, the seller's whim being perhaps sobered a little by his memory of old competitive rates. Slowly, caprice gives way to law; but it is a new law—that of men's need. In other words, the tolerance of the market now governs price. Prices go higher and higher till demand, and hence profit, begins to fall off; and they then play about the line of what the market will bear, much as they used to play about that of cost. The producer can be more or less exacting according to the nature of the product. If it is a luxury, he may not be able to elevate prices greatly above the old notch. If it is a necessity, he may bleed people to death.

The price cannot, of course, permanently fall below the cost of production; but, if the monopoly is close and the article one of necessity, it may indefinitely exceed cost. In rare cases this might occur with a luxury. Should fashion create among the wealthy an intense desire for Constantia wine, a pipe of it costing $100 might sell for $100,000. Let Constantia become indispensable to life, and the ratio of selling price to cost would be vastly greater than that.

This contention is not invalidated by the fact that few if any of the combinations now existing have as yet raised prices up to the full tolerance of the market. There are many reasons why they have not. But that it will be done in due time, provided these powerful embodiments of capital are left unbridled to the play of mere economic law, is as sure as fate.

Trusts threaten the people with a graver evil than that of exorbitant prices,—that of apathy toward industrial improvements and inventions and tardiness in adopting such. Competition has been a keen spur to the betterment of methods in production. The danger is that now, so soon as all the production in a given line comes under a single management, old methods will be thought sufficient and kept in use long after competition would have cast them aside.

To realize the seriousness of this peril we must remember that the present state of things,—in which, owing to the existence, still, of alert would-be rivals in their business, even the firmest monopolies neglect improvements at their peril—cannot always last. That mighty motive to improvement must at length cease to act. The evil confronting us will then be not an army of combines knowing that all sorts of bettered methods are abroad yet stubbornly refusing to adopt them, but a downright dearth of invention and inventiveness due to lack of incentive. I cannot but think that in this important regard the system of trusts is obnoxious to the same criticism nearly always made against socialism.

Another momentous and threatening change must attend the general marshaling of industries in companies and battalions. This marshaling is to bring with it a subordination of men to men, of the many to the few, more complete than has ever prevailed since feudalism. It will introduce in effect a new feudalism, with the chance that in the new, lords and vassals will be very lacking in the mutual love and sense of mutual responsibility prevalent under the old. Nor does it appear how long a political democracy that shall be more than a name, can endure in face of such an aristocratic industrial organization.

Monopoly may work injustice without appearing to do so. The law of monopoly price shows its full significance only when industry is considered dynamically. Whereas a *régime* of competition inevitably tends to throw into the lap of consumers all the benefits arising from improved processes in production, monopoly tends to retain all these in producers' hands. It may thus come to pass that, even when prices experience no absolute rise, or even fall a few points, they still range far above what they would have been if governed by competition, the producer pocketing all the gains afforded by new inventions in machinery and methods, whether made by himself or by others.

In a case like this, the circumstance that prices have not risen makes it specially easy to deceive the public. The profits, how exorbitant soever, are not likely to be published, and the fact that they arise more or less at the expense of all of us, since now, though we pay no higher than formerly, we still do pay more than we should have had to pay with competition, is too recondite for popular attention. Press and platform echo the praises of such a monopoly, when it may in fact be a much worse leech upon the body politic than another which, having elevated prices a little absolutely, is deafened with a perfect diapason of anathema.

If the lessened cost of the article is entirely due to the monopoly, or to the skill and exertions of those who profit thereby, many will be of the opinion that the monopolists have a right to all the gains thus arising. Massed capital and centralized control are tremendous advantages, and may be made vastly to cheapen production. Ought not those to reap the gains who render possible these better conditions of industry? Ought not society gladly to acquiesce in an arrangement, though perhaps excessively profitable to a few, which furnishes it a given line of products as cheaply as competition ever did?

This is a very important ethical question. Its bearings are too manifold for full discussion here. Permit a remark or two, however. Monopolists often utilize, to swell their own dividends, improvements which they had no hand whatever in originating, and of which they have gotten the control by the most doubtful means. To the proceeds of these society has as good a claim as they.

Again, it seems clear that society's right, whether enforcible or otherwise, to participate in the advantages which the bettered means of production in any department afford, is not cut off at the limit which invention had reached when the monopoly was established. Some advancement would surely have been made had competition continued. This would then naturally have accrued to the weal of all of us; and the use of any means to thwart such a result would have been denounced as an infringement of our rights. If that judgment would have been just, the public is justified in demanding at least that share in the present profits of any form of production now monopolized which would have fallen to it had not the monopoly arisen. Hence, even if we limit society's right in the manner just indicated, the mere truth that a monopoly has not elevated prices is no proof that its riches have not been gotten in part at the expense of consumers.

But I, for one, should not always agree to this limitation of the social claim, since, though an existing monopoly may have effected colossal saving, as much as you please beyond what would have been possible with competition, and may have shared these gains with the public so as to lower prices a little, it does not appear but that a different private monopoly or control by the state itself might have done for the public far better still. Patent rights are limited, however probable it may now and then be that but for the patentee the improvement would never have been made.

The plea is sometimes interposed that no harm can come to people in general, let monopoly profits be never so high, for the reason that the winners cannot possibly keep to themselves what they get. The wealth cannot remain piled up, it is said, but the very motive which prompted the amassing of it must lead to the spending of it; and this cannot take place without a wide and rich dissemination of its benefits.

Such as find comfort in this thought are very easily

pleased. The same logic could be employed to justify the creation of financial princes by taxation outright. Any such policy would desperately discourage wealth-creation, even if every cent of the vast piles were to be productively spent. The greater part might be invested abroad — profitably for owners, at little less than dead loss to their fellow-citizens. But a generally lucrative employment of so great wealth, either at home or abroad, could not be expected. Excessive incomes, save in rarest cases, however thriftily intentioned their recipients may be, cannot be invested in the wisest manner. But economists are forced to observe that inordinate wealth almost inevitably tends to impair thrift, leading its possessors to prefer unproductive to productive forms of expenditure.

There is hope that combination in industry may, after all, become an immense net advantage to humanity.

While it is unfortunately true that the central control of each great business must dull the old spur to improvements in production, it is to be noticed that combinations open vast possibilities of improvement which, if another motive to the utilizing of them can be in any way provided, will change the world. In illustration of these new possibilities, I need refer only to the pipe line system for transporting crude petroleum, the colossal scale on which cotton seed is now pressed, the tank steamers which carry oil across the ocean, the glorious and successful campaign of market-making in which the two oil trusts are engaging in Europe and

Asia, and the lucrative by-industries which these as well as the Sugar Trust carry on. For stupendous undertakings like these competition was utterly inadequate.

Combination's benign power in coördinating industry is manifest in another sphere. Socialists have said none too much about the destructive cross purposes and lack of system which of necessity prevailed when production was unregulated. Let the business man be as careful as he may, under the style of business once prevalent he cannot but take most dangerous risks. Competition offers but the roughest means for ascertaining what the next season's demand for this or that line of goods is to be, and still fainter hints touching the output to be expected from one's rivals. Amid such uncertainty, every year's operation of a manufactory is to a great extent a game of hazard. Prices fluctuate abnormally, deranging and discouraging industry. Lines of business are over-wrought, begetting glut and necessitating sales below cost; needless plant is set out, which must decay or burn. Losses in these ways are beyond computation, and so much more sad in that they might be avoided. Through such waste of capital interest rises, and wage-yielding businesses which might have flourished are prevented from starting.

The prevention and destruction of wealth in these ways are great enough to make some economists doubt whether the trust-system does not, at its worst, effect for society some net saving. I do not think it as yet benefits society thus; but it is very certain that in this matter of preventing haphazard and amorphous production trusts compass vast economy for some one. They forcast the demand and regulate supply accordingly, much as would occur under socialism. Then, in providing the needed store, massed capital and centralized control offer incalculable advantages over the old, go-as-you-please way of producing. That the intrinsic cost of commodities turned out by organized industry is less than cost would be under competitive production no one can deny. The question is, how much, if any, of the saving thus effected finds its way into consumers' pockets. The point for society to aim at is to continue all the advantages of monopoly, increasing them if possible, while preventing the monopolists themselves from going to sleep or retaining more than their just share of what they make. Society wishes to utilize the trust with all its actual and possible economies in production, and to devise some means, as efficient as competition used to be, for breeding inventiveness and for draining into its own till all the savings of all business after paying producers the cost of production plus a generous profit.

Three schemes for doing this have been proposed: first, socialism; second, the assumption by the state of all monopolized production; and third, regulation.

The first, socialism, is simply the system of trusts made universal, all land and productive wealth belonging to the one, great, all-inclusive trust, and every citizen being in effect a holder of trust certificates.

Trusts and Other Combinations of Capital   47

This plan would be attended with many and insuperable difficulties, which it is impossible to review in this place.

It has also been proposed, in order to secure to society the benefits of massed capital under central management, that the state assume, not indeed all industries without exception, but all such as naturally take on the monopoly-form. Advocates of this policy usually have in mind businesses like railroads, the telegraph, and mines, those, that is, which never have been and cannot be subject to competition.

Whatever reasons there have been heretofore, in a discussion like ours, for distinguishing these from the other substantive industries of the civilized world, there is none now. All are or are soon to be monopolized. The proposal under consideration would, then, practically amount to socialism, which, as just remarked, is not to be thought of except as a fate. I have no doubt, for my part, that many industries now in private hands will sooner or later be bought by the public power, and I would unhesitatingly vote for thus dealing with any one of them so soon as it proved defiant or subversive of the general good. Until this is clearly the case with any given one, regulation should be the method of dealing with it rather than assumption.

Many socialists themselves admit that, till men are morally better, grave dangers must attend any enlargement of state participation in industry. That policy gives scope for cheating; it is apt to render workmen indolent; and it narrows the field for invention and other splendid forms of personal initiative. It is not wise, then, for the state to undertake industry faster than this is necessary for public protection. Try regulation in every case until it certainly fails. No systematic effort to regulate monopolies in the public interest has yet been made except in the case of the railways, and even there the effort is as yet none too serious. We shall become serious in this endeavor soon, and carry it further. Nothing would be easier, in most industries, than to insure the public against wrongs while at the same time avoiding all injustice to stockholders and bondholders. We should be as careful to do no wrong as to suffer none.

But supposing that we can rely upon the regulation of massed industry by public authority to shield us from robbery in the form of exorbitant prices, where shall we look for that spur to the invention of improved machinery and processes which have been the glory of competitive industry? And what is going to put such a spirit into the coming feudalism as may render it a blessing or at least save it from being a curse? Society wants all the good which banded industry can bring it through the agency of great capital and orderly control; but these benefits alone will not compensate for the loss of civil liberty or for the decadence of genius in invention and initiative. If the new age of industry is to advance humanity instead of causing retrogression, something must come with it that shall conserve freedom and enterprise. If the solidarity of industry is in store, as I believe to be the case, unless it is to bring some such preservative accompaniment, the outlook is gloomy indeed. What can we hope?

That is a question which political economy does not answer. It brings us to one of the very numerous points where political economy abuts upon ethics. That the approaching industrial age may carry our dear humanity a step nearer its millenium, moral betterment must come to men. We must have more philanthropy, richer, more solid character, willingness in men to do for love what hitherto only money could induce. Nor is this humanity's imbroglio here alone. At every point, economic advance, increase in temporal good, waits, in last analysis, upon spiritual advance, increase in moral good.

Let us recapitulate.

We have seen that the competitive system of industry is fast giving way to one of combination; that this is not due in any extent to legislation, but springs out of stringent social laws; that solidarity in industry often exists when it does not appear; that such solidarity is not a transitory phenomenon, but destined to be permanent; that this monopolistic form of industrial organization has in it the power to work society great evil; that it often produces ill consequences without appearing to do so; that there is, indeed, hope after all of its bringing to society immense net advantages; but that no such happy result can come save on the condition of men's moral improvement.

III

ECONOMIC EVILS AS AIDED BY LEGISLATION

THE evils discussed in this lecture differ in an essential particular from any that are due to Combinations of Capital. Their main, their most grievous pressure upon society springs not from mere industrial evolution, as trusts do, but from perverse legislation or lack of legislation. In this category come bad taxation, bad land laws, and the vices of our monetary system.

Endless injustice arises from the endeavor, apparently so proper when superficially considered, to tax each particular species and article of property. This "distributive" taxation is unfortunately, as yet, the American ideal. So early as May, 1634, the General Court of Massachusetts ordered that in all rates and public charges the town should "have respect to levy every man according to his estate and with consideration of all other of his abilities whatsoever." The other States have nearly all adopted the same principle, and it has come to form the main basis of state and local taxation throughout the Union.

But experience proves this venerable rule of distributiveness in taxing to be thoroughly bad. It worked well enough in colonial days, when almost all property was tangible and bulky, and therefore hard to be concealed. It will not do to-day, when towards half of the nation's wealth is personal property, and the most valuable part of this, viz., paper titles, easily hidden. The inevitable latter day operation of the plan is to foster dishonesty, to fine and discourage public spirit, to rob the defenceless and the poor, and to aid extraordinarily wealthy people in evading their fair allotment of fiscal dues.

Of the valuable papers which should by law pay taxes, only a beggarly proportion is in fact reached, and the result is not greatly better in the bulky forms of personalty. There is no doubt that in New York and New England the personal estate would upon an equitable rating prove equal in value to the real. The proportion of real, moreover, grows each year. But the assessor finds the one and more and more misses the other. In 1869 New York State derived only 78 per cent. of its revenue from realty, 22 per cent. from personalty. In 1879, realty paid 87.8 per cent., personalty only 12.2 per cent. The more recent returns tell the same story: personal property increases, both relatively and absolutely, faster than real, but pays a smaller and smaller share of the taxes. The same occurs in Rhode Island. In the urban communities of that commonwealth, real estate was assessed in 1887 for 18¾ million dollars more than in 1877; personal estate for $279,669 less. Boston, in 1884, assessed its realty at $488,130,-600, its personalty only at $194,526,050; these sums representing a gain in realty of $32,442,000 from 1881 to 1884, and a loss in (assessed) personalty during the same years of $15,639,939.

Lest it should be thought that securities alone thus elude assessment, I name one case out of many which could be cited. Pennsylvania lays a tax of $1 each on gold watches, of $0.75 each on silver watches, of $0.50 each on other watches. Following are the numbers of watches actually assessed against the (nearly) 1,000,000 people of Philadelphia for the years named:*

	1883.	1884.	1885.
Gold watches,	14,515	18,509	18,390
Silver watches,	375	675	545
Other watches,	19	74	55

If the extra taxation unfairly entailed by these exemptions were a mere thing of chance, likely to injure one man now, another next time, the evil would be comparatively slight. Instead of that the injustice always lights where even justice would be severe — on widows, orphans, the insane, and the poor. All trust funds, nearly, are so invested or deposited that the assessors cannot but list them, and at their full value. Since so many lie or otherwise defraud, all who will not or who cannot do so are absolutely certain to be overtaxed.

It will occur to many to suggest as the sole needed remedy for such wrongs, stronger integrity in assessors. This would help greatly. A leading member of the New York State Convention of 1867-8 said: "There is

---

* Ely, "Taxation in American States and Cities."

not an assessment roll now made out in this State which does not both work and tell lies." Cases of collusion by assessors with wealthy taxpayers are painfully common. Equally so are cases where honest assessors have failed of election through the hostility of those from whom they had exacted justice.

But the evil is too radical to be overcome by assessors, however good. The iniquity often has its source in the very dutifulness of these officials. The 1872 Report of the New York State Tax Commission relates this: During the war a worthy farmer in Central New York, growing old, sold for $5,000 his hard-earned estate, accepting a mortgage for most of the sum, and expecting the interest to support himself and wife during their declining years. The transaction being well known, the mortgage was assessed at its full value. That very year the town voted large money to avoid a draft — to which the old man was not liable — raising taxation to a figure beyond the legal rate of interest, and forcing the aged couple, in order to meet their taxes, to go out at days' work. This, while the mortgaged farm was taxed at 1-5 its full value, and in a state whose personality at large was at that time taxed for a sum far less than the aggregate fortunes of its 30 wealthiest citizens.

Not infrequently, too, new rigor of assessment in a given city has driven capital thence to localities known to be more lax. And how could assessors prevent the habit, so general among the wealthy, of fixing their legal residences, the *situs*, of course, for taxing their personalty, in country places, where the rates are low, leaving to the less favored people in town, who cannot afford duplicate residences, to pay extra in order to protect the town properties of such as can?

The decisive difficulty lies in the total, hopeless impossibility of collecting taxes on all the numberless items of personal property. No human power or art can do it. The effort, long since abandoned in England as hopeless, we ought at once and for ever to give up. To tax realty alone would be far fairer than our present method. Land and buildings cannot be hidden, and intelligent and honest endeavor could not fail to make assessments on them reasonably just. Then, through the operation of the principle known as the "repercussion" of taxes, burdens upon realty would with a close approach to equity be transferred in due measure to holders of personal estate. Repercussion will not, as some suppose, render just any and every form of tax. Were we, for instance, to raise all our revenues from a tax on labor, laborers could only to a little extent shift the load to others' shoulders. But a realty tax, since all live from land, and all dwell or do business in buildings, could and would be felt by all.

The corrective which Henry George and his growing army of followers propose for the bad state of things pointed out is the single land tax; and they have much to say in favor of their proposal. But, before broaching that matter, I ought, in justice both to Mr. George and to the subject, to show how he becomes interested in taxation. I therefore lay upon the table for a few minutes the subject of taxation, and bring forward the second main topic of this lecture, that of the injustice connected with the private owning of land. To redress this injustice, not to remedy fiscal outrages, is Mr. George's primary aim. He sees our land-tenure system enriching some men without desert and impoverishing others without ill-desert. Casting about for relief from this unfairness, he seems to find such in a new plan of taxation; yet his interest in this is due solely to his wish for justice in the matter of land-holding.

While not agreeing with Mr. George in details, touching either the disease which he describes or the cure by him proposed, I cannot but think that he has unveiled a flagrant wrong; and the nature of this I wish now to make clear.

As population grows in any country or vicinity, less and less desirable land has to be brought under cultivation, viz., that which is either naturally less fertile or more remote from centres of population. The price of the new product must of course be sufficiently high to render remunerative this more difficult production. By a well-known law, the cost of production on these least economic tracts, in other words, the dearest cost of production, determines the selling price of all the produce now demanded, whether raised upon the land long cultivated or upon that newly put to use. But, since the cost of production on the older and more convenient areas has not been in the slightest degree raised by the increase of population and of production, the owners of those most favored tracts now possess a bonanza. With them, cost of production no longer bears any relation to selling price. They may sell produce for double, treble, or quadruple what it cost them. The only limit to their gains is the pressure of population. Speaking generally, every acre of land under cultivation is rendered more valuable by every advance in population. The new-comers must be supplied with food, to produce which is a more and more difficult business. All food, therefore, rises in value, and all holders of land in cultivation reap the benefits.

The statement just made is, in brief, the doctrine of economic rent. All that income which a given acre of land yields, over and above the income derived from the poorest acre which has to be cultivated in order to supply the market, is the rent of that acre. The price of wheat being, say, $1.00 a bushel, fixed at that by the cost of production on the worst acre which the market at a given time requires to be tilled, I, owning land from which a bushel can be put upon the market for fifty cents, have a gratuitous advantage of fifty cents a bushel over my handicapped competitor. If an acre of my land produces twenty bushels of wheat, its rent is ten dollars per acre. This is what all careful writers upon the subject mean by economic rent: the returns that come to a land-owner not from what he has done on, to, or for his land, but from the presence and labors of the surrounding population.

In cities and towns the truth of rent applies to building lots just as in agricultural sections it applies to farm land. To get rich, you have only to own land in a growing town. You need not toil or spin. Travel, sleep, study; it matters not which you do; your wealth multiplies apace. Every new resident, every new business coming to town puts money in your purse, tending to push up the price of lots suitable for building, yours with the rest.

All Manhattan Island was first purchased for sixty guilders, about $24. On the main street-fronts of New York City that sum would to-day not purchase half a foot. In 1886, store sites on Fifth Avenue cost $65 per square foot. On Broad Street, $85 per foot has been paid; on Broadway, $100 and $115. Some shares of a land company at Birmingham, Ala., costing $1,100, recently paid a yearly dividend of $24,000. In London land has often sold for $240 per foot, and select spots, it is said, for as much as it would cost to pave them with sovereigns laid upon edge.

It should be particularly noticed that this mounting up of land values is the result of the community's labor. It is no unmediated gift of Providence; it does not come by chance. Men toil for it. But,—and here is the wrong that evokes Henry George's reprobation —this peculiar value does not accrue to the behoof of the men who by their labor cause it, the toilers, the industrious public at large, but goes to swell the pile of this or that party who merely happens to own it. Such man may, indeed, as one of a million, have done something to build such value, but frequently not even so much can be said. The owner may never have done anything to give rise to this or to any other wealth. He may be an absentee landlord or a foreigner out and out. At best, his equitable interest in the property must be infinitesimally small. That makes no difference. By our present law this increment in land value goes to him, not to us who created it. To the community it is earned increment; to the owner it is unearned increment. He has reaped where he did not sow and gathered where he did not strew. A land-law system hailing all the way from ancient Rome, originating when there was land enough and to spare for all, thus makes it possible for individuals and private corporations to gain and hold a mighty bulk of mammon which in equity belongs to the entire industrial body.

The value of property other than land, as a house or a store in a populous quarter, is no doubt sometimes affected with unearned increment, accruing to private wealth; but in such cases the value to which the addition was made, the core about which it grew, was of private creation. Besides, the total of values arising in this way is insignificant as compared with corresponding land values. That incidental unearned gains should, on the basis of private industry, go to enrich the subjects of such industry is a light matter; but it is not a light thing that laws should place to the private account of individuals and corporations a vast category of the nation's wealth which the beneficiaries have done nothing whatever to earn.

Just as values of things besides land may receive

unearned increment, extensive value may be given to land itself by private industry. This occurs when a land company improves a locality so as to make it desirable for residence or business. The co-operators in such circumstances are not likely in a long time to reap more than they have sown, though it is conceivable that they should ultimately do so.

A most remarkable instance of this sort is that of the Pecos Valley Land Company, whose headquarters are at Colorado Springs. Under the energetic and skillful management of Mr. J. J. Hagerman, that organization has arranged to irrigate a vast territory in New Mexico, taking it when practically a desert waste and making it literally blossom as the rose. Its value bids fair to be decupled at least, and it may be decupled ten times over. That this enhancement of value belongs to its creators, not to the public, is as obvious as it is that such increments generally belong of right not to corporations or to individuals but to the whole of us.

We may now recur to Henry George, who means to kill with his one stone, the single tax, both the noxious birds just described, that of vicious taxation and that of iniquitous land tenure.

I have long been convinced that the break between land and people by the general prevalence of Roman or feudal land law has become a terrible evil, and that it operates much as Henry George describes, diminishing production, congesting wealth, and multiplying injustice, poverty, and vice. An increasing number of able English and American writers share this view;

and it is masterfully argued in much the most considerable economic work of this decade, Achille Loria's "Analysis of Property under the Capitalist Régime," published at Turin year before last. To turn the golden stream of economic rent partly or mostly into the state's treasury, where it would relieve the public of taxation in burdensome forms, seems to me extraordinarily desirable. I by no means concur in all the reasons which many assign for this; nor should I expect from it, even if carried to Mr. George's length, more than half the benefits to society which he anticipates? Still, the proposition that the state ought to lay its main tax on land impresses me as just, safe, accordant with the best canons of public finance, and, in fact, every way excellent.

But I, for my part, should deprecate an absolutely single tax system of any sort, the more if the one tax were upon land. When, a few years since, Professor Harris and Mr. Atkinson, referring to the United States, and Mr. Richard Simon, with reference to Great Britain, held forth that the economic rent of the nation's land would not suffice for its revenue, I was anxious to agree with them, though I could not. It occurred to me that, if they were right, we could beautifully remedy the evils of *latifundia*, land dearth and speculation, without entirely ceasing to draw public revenue from other sources than rent.

I suppose, however, that, as a fact, rent would pay all our taxes and leave a vast sum remaining. Were the state to take it all, the fund would be greater than

Economic Evils as Aided by Legislation 61

it could safely disburse, inducing subventions to all sorts of people, which could not but work detriment to their economic character. On the other hand, should the state not take the whole surplus rent, the evils attaching to our land tenure, instead of being cured, would simply be more or less assuaged. I should, however, prefer this as far the lesser misfortune. To collect unnecessary revenue is, in finance, the unpardonable sin; and it would in the end work as ill socially as it would financially.

There are other objections to the plan of deriving all public revenue from a tax upon land alone. It would aggravate the wrong of all imperfections in assessment, which are unavoidable whatever system of taxation is followed. It would produce a most inelastic fiscal system. It would take from our hands a much needed weapon for disciplining minatory and refractory businesses. And it would gravely threaten free institutions. This last count deserves a word of amplification.

The operation of the single tax in the form desired by Mr. George provides government with the most ample revenues in a dangerously silent, imperceptible, and automatic manner. The system once launched, the state waxes rich, sleeping or waking, like landlords in growing cities. Increased revenue comes without debate or observation. No budget is presented or discussed. Public assessors, incessantly but noiselessly at work, ascertain and register each rise in land value, while collectors, at once and without ado, drain the additional rent into the public till. Of course, the individuals who have this year to pay more rent-tax than last are aware of the difference and may complain. But such voices, being without volume or unity because isolated, would have no effect. There could be no common consciousness of drain. Unless all political experience is at fault, let government thus have access to ample resources which are not voted to it item by item after debate and reflection, and liberty will soon be but a name.

It would be my thought, then, not to tax land alone, yet I would draw the state's main revenue from a land tax. Ninety per cent. of all public moneys needed might, I should think, be well taken from that source. It would be the fairest tax imaginable, both as coming from a fund created by the same public who would utilize it, and as susceptible of the utmost attainable equity in assessment and collection. By leaving ten per cent. of the needed revenue to be raised in other ways we should avoid all the dangers of the single tax.

We could very easily use the power of taxation to bring to terms lawless combinations of capital. When any monopoly has made the prices of its products as high as the market will bear, if it is required to pay the public in taxes a round per cent. of its winnings, it is powerless to collect any part of this levy from its customers by raising prices. It must settle its tax bill out of its profits. Here is a splendid opportunity for exercising public discipline over any capitalistic organizations which need such.

We have thus seen how, by throwing the leading tax

Economic Evils as Aided by Legislation   63

upon land, securing from the rent of land, deriving from the unearned increment of land value the chief part of the state's revenue, we can at one stroke abate the principal evils of land-holding and of taxation both, while not introducing any other evils in their stead.

I hasten to introduce the third matter proposed for discussion in this lecture, the world's vicious system of hard money.

Unless allied with silver money upon an equality, gold money is not equitable or honest money, but is continually and inevitably a source of fraud between man and man. I am for hard money, money of the very solidest sort, but I demand a species of hard money that will not work injustice. Every debt ought to be paid in gold or its equivalent, but gold ought to be joined with silver so as not to gain or lose in value between contract-day and pay-day. To prevent this result a system of money is necessary in which the amount of money shall be plentiful enough to keep prices from falling, yet not sufficiently abundant to make them rise, it being an economic law that prices rise and fall in more or less regular accord with increase or shrinkage in the volume of money.* If there is not money enough, prices fall; if there is too much, they rise. Stability of general

---

* Strictly the money which determines prices is full, final, fundamental, or exportable money, money of the kind which will do whatever the best money can do. Much inferior money may be in circulation and even be kept at par with the best, without having full monetary effect in sustaining prices.

prices is the one infallible test of the question whether a population is properly supplied with money.

Judged by this criterion, which, I repeat, is the only correct one, the gold-using world has been short of full money ever since silver was demonetized by Germany in 1873. That act, in which Germany was followed by Holland and Scandinavia, led France and the states in monetary covenant with her to suspend the coinage of silver, and the United States greatly to limit it. In a word, since that date silver has ceased to be, as it had till then been through all history, the mate and peer of gold in the world's trade. The part of the world which was far the most important industrially lost something like half of its basal money at once, and that at a moment when its business and population were rapidly increasing. At the same time the annual product of gold from the mines fell off, so that now a sum nearly or quite equal to the whole of this product is each year used in the arts, leaving little or none to be added to the circulation. It was inevitable that prices should fall. The wonder is that they have not fallen fifty per cent. instead of thirty.

Now, one of the very worst evils of the legal sort which we are surveying in this lecture, laws making some men rich at others' expense and wholly apart from economic merit, is this fluctuation in the purchasing power of money. It is peculiarly bad because it is sweeping in its operation, and also because it works so silently and subtly that only the trained mind can see what is doing. If general prices fall, holders of money and of titles calling for money grow rich by cutting coupons, taking to themselves so much of society's pile for no equivalent whatever, of course making the rest in like degree poorer. If general prices rise, the reverse infelicity occurs. It is quite immaterial whether the fatal change in the value of money arises from new plenty or new scarcity of money itself, or because of extra dearness or cheapness of cost on the part of general commodities. It is as truly a source of robbery in the one case as in the other.

Were money merely a medium of exchange, something to be spoken into being for each act of traffic, and then annihilated, permanence in its worth could be dispensed with. But money also, besides mediating exchanges, serves as a standard for deferred payments. To fulfil this office ideally or even justly it must preserve its general purchasing power unchanged from period to period. Increase in the value of money (falling prices) robs debtors. It forces every one of them to pay more than he covenanted — not more dollars but more value, the given number of dollars embodying at date of payment greater value than at date of contract. Decrease in the value of money (rising prices) robs creditors, compelling each to put up, in payment of what is due him, with a smaller modicum of value than was agreed upon.

Such losses, whichever the direction of their incidence, are a misfortune not only ethically, but also economically. They are so much friction against the natural and desirable free play of exchange among men.

In case money gains in power over commodities, so that prices fall, a quite special degree of this friction is experienced. Under such circumstances money and titles to money become rich forms of property to hold, apart from the interest upon them, that is, apart from the use of them. Money is thus no longer freely exchanged, as it should be, for other forms of capital, but is either hoarded or loaned to such as can thoroughly assure its return in kind. This baneful effect, painfully discouraging industry and production, has had more to do than any other one thing in creating the hard times of recent years.

When general prices are falling, or, what is only another way of expressing the same truth, when the value of money is increasing, there is a very special risk in undertaking to produce. To produce, one must for the time let go his money. One must *invest* in some form of property, say, a mill, some machinery, and some stock to work up into goods. But, if prices are falling, such an investment is nearly certain to lose in value while on one's hands. Unless he has some special "pull" upon society, so that he can charge arbitrarily for his wares, the man either never gets his money back, or gets it back with far less profit than he anticipated. Thousands of men, able, careful, earnest, trying to do business while prices are falling, find their resources growing less and less each time they are turned over, until at last failure and poverty result.

Just as productive industry is painfully discouraged by falling prices, the holding of money and of titles calling for money, is unfortunately encouraged. In times of falling prices, to hold money, or to loan it out on such gilt-edged security that it cannot help returning to your hands, is profitable quite independently of and away beyond any interest which it may bring. Each grain of gold, or piece of paper certainly redeemable in gold, waxes more and more precious by the simple lapse of time, whether you put it to use or not.

Falling prices, therefore, always mean the discouragement of production on the one hand, and the hoarding of money on the other, both of which effects are most deleterious, since what society needs is that the production of wealth should be promoted in every possible way.

The demonetization of silver, then, and the consequent advance in the value of gold, has had the pernicious results of tainting with injustice every time-contract made anywhere in the gold-using world since 1873, and of afflicting with paralysis all productive industry throughout the same vast area, so that the world's wealth is to-day less by billions than it would be had normal monetary conditions been enjoyed.

More than this, the demonetization of silver has split the commercial earth in two, into a gold-employing and a silver-employing hemisphere, between which, so great is the difficulty of exchange, commerce has ceased to be a rational affair and has become in effect a game of hazard. Thus, in another way, have the growth of wealth and the advance of civilization been retarded. And, last, by thus deranging international exchanges, the disuse of silver as full money has discouraged and, to a colossal extent, lessened in amount the loaning of capital by rich countries to poor, indefinitely to the disadvantage of both, so, by still another method, hindering the weal and progress of mankind.

The aim of this lecture has been to show the desirableness of placing upon land the main, or a much larger tax than it now bears, and of restoring silver to the full monetary function which it had always enjoyed before 1873. This cannot be done by any one nation alone. An international compact is required. A system of taxation may be national; but there can be, strictly, no such thing as a national system of money, any more than there can be one of air.*

---

*See the writer's article on "Tariff Reform and Monetary Reform," in the *North American Review* for April, 1894.

IV

ECONOMIC EVILS DUE TO SOCIAL CONDITIONS

THIS lecture continues the discussion of the faults, wrongs, and dislocations characteristic of the present economic *régime*, but without particular regard to the question whether such infelicities have their immediate source in legislation, in the nature of society, or in men's selfishness and perversity.

I speak first of *gambling*. Of this there are numerous forms, many of them so clearly evil that one need not stop to brand them so. Lotteries, once so common, patronized and promoted by the best people, all now see to be unqualifiedly bad. More toleration is accorded to private gambling at cards, roulette, faro, and the like; yet none would be found, I think, to champion such practices as of other than vicious and baneful tendency. There is also a healthy and widespread inclination to discountenance pool-selling and book-making in their various forms.

The sort of gambling which fails of due condemnation, not being sufficiently understood, is gambling in the form of betting on "futures" in various stocks and commodities. It is, in a word, business gambling. The main reason why people do not see the wrong of this is that in some of its forms it is only in the keenest analysis distinguished from legitimate speculation. It is by those who engage in it always styled "speculation"—a euphemism like that of New York thieves and pickpockets, who, Mr. Riis says, never speak of having "stolen" a watch or other valuable; they have "won" it. People not gamblers contribute to this confusion and to the prevalence of gambling by stigmatizing all speculation as gambling.

In this they err. There is speculation which is right and proper, advantageous to the entire community. Suppose a real buyer of actual goods wishes the goods to use in his own business, yet, without "rigging" the market in any way, buys them before he needs them, believing that when needed they will have become dearer. That is speculation, but, far from having done any harm, it has demonstrably done general good.

Take another case. The dealer buys *bona fide*, as before, intending to own the goods and to hold them for a rise, although he does not mean to consume them for himself, but to sell them so soon as he can do this with sufficient profit. Here, too, is speculation, but, if the man does nothing to "rig" the market, his act bears no uneconomic or immoral quality whatever. He has robbed no one, hurt no one.

I give you an illustration of this. Just after the war some American cotton speculators, convinced that the article would soon rise, bought a vast amount of cotton which was about to be exported to Europe, and soon sold it to American manufacturers at a snug advance.

They got rich, but did good. Our manufacturers bought cotton of them much cheaper than they could have obtained it if they had had to re-import; the planters received more than England was going to pay them; the cost of two freightings across the Atlantic was saved; and the speculative profits remained in this country.

We can see that proper speculation always tends to be advantageous. It acts like a governor to a steam engine, preventing prices from rising so high or falling so low as they otherwise would. Shocks in the market that but for it would be terrible are so distributed by it as to render them least harmful. The effect of absolutely wise speculation would be to annihilate speculation. Honest speculation is, therefore, negatively productive, like the work of judges, army, and police; it is not creative of wealth, but preventive of loss. Gambling manifestly lacks this saving character. It does not steady prices, but the reverse. At best, it but transfers property from pocket to pocket.

There need also be nothing wrong in buying or selling an "option" or a "future," if only real business is in question. To buy out-and-out for future delivery is sometimes a necessity of every great business. You, being a dealer in actual·cotton, agree to deliver me 100 bales of the fibre next July 1, and I, actually wishing to purchase, agree to pay you so much a pound. Who can object to such a transaction? But I may not be sure of needing the cotton, in which case I covenant with you to deliver it for so much in case I desire it, though I need not take it unless I wish. That is an "option," and, provided actual business is at its basis—provided, that is, I am a real manufacturer or jobber, and actually liable to want cotton on July 1, fully intending to acquire this lot if my business is so and so—then the "option," like the simple "future," is no form of gambling, and is not immoral.

Nor do I see any intrinsic or necessary harm in buying or selling "on margin," as it is called, in case all the transactions are *bona fide*. I go to a broker, wishing actually to deal in a given stock; he actually buys for me some of that stock, though I pay him but in part, viz., his "margin," agreeing to pay him the rest when he sells. If the stock rises, I gain, and may have something left after settling with my broker; if it falls, I lose, the broker recouping himself for his outlay and labor from what the stock brings, plus my margin money, and being careful to sell before it is too late thus to make himself whole.

Still further, if one wishes and intends really to trade, I see no more objection to his selling "short" than I do to his holding for a rise.

What, then, is gambling speculation? It is buying or selling without the power or the disposition to bring about any transfer of real goods at all; it is selling what you do not own, or buying what you do not expect or wish to acquire; it is going through the form of purchase and sale, without any thought of actual goods or actual trade; it is just betting on the future prices of things.

With no purpose to deliver, I buy of you the privilege of delivering you 100 shares of stock or barrels of beef a month hence at a specified price, my belief being that the then price will be less than the one specified. That is a "put." Not wanting any goods, I still buy of you the privilege of receiving some then at a given price — *i. e.*, you agree to deliver them to me. That is a "call." Or I may buy of you the privilege of either delivering to you, or getting from you, — the privilege of selling to you or buying from you certain valuables, at a certain price, within such a time. That would be a "spread," a "spread eagle," or a "straddle." Each of these, according to the aspect of the case, might be an "option," a "future," or a "privilege."

Any of these operations may be gone through with legitimately. They are all proper if based upon reality. But mostwise they are not so based. They are in the air, having no more to do with the real values specified in them than with the stars. This is why they usually constitute gambling, pure and simple.

No doubt the line between legitimacy and illegitimacy in these affairs may sometimes be well-nigh invisible. I may actually purchase 1,000 barrels of pork, but, not wishing it at once, may get it housed for a time in the seller's warehouse. Before it is touched he may wish to re-purchase it, to which, of course, none can object. Here is no physical transfer of goods. Not a barrel of the commodity has stirred an inch. How does the case differ from transactions which I have denounced as vicious? In this — that there was here an intended and a real legal transfer; there was veritable trading. Both dealers' minds were occupied with tangible goods.

A single case of the kind suggested might offer no proof of the superiority of *bona fide* trade to sham trade in its influence upon the community. Yet it is not hard to see this superiority when one compares a million cases of the one kind with a million cases of the other. In true trade men tend to study markets, to acquaint themselves with the facts of production, exchange, and consumption in the fields which they touch. They, therefore, tend to buy and sell in such ways as to check fluctuations in prices. In sham trade it is not so. If the statement that such make-believe dealers utterly ignore factual markets would be too strong, certain it is that the course of real trade is among the last considerations which they raise. Their business bears no calculable relation to the facts of the economic world. In Chicago, in 1882, three hundred billion dollars' worth of nominal sales occurred, when the whole real produce exchanged was less than $400,000,000 in value. Such nominal business does not aid in forecasting the course of prices, but goes far to make this impossible. It does not steady prices, but is one of the most potent forces in unsteadying them.

I say, therefore, that business gambling, sham speculation, nominal trading which leaves actual values out of view, differs in no moral particular from gaming at faro, roulette, or bluff. It contributes to a popular

Economic Evils due to Social Conditions 75

gambling mania which causes infinite loss, poverty, and misery; he who engages in it toys with the stability of his character in its most delicate parts; and, further, so far as he gains livelihood or fortune from this source, as many do, his gain is theft, being at the expense of his fellow-men, a taking from society with no return.

The subject of gambling naturally brings up that of *corporations*, for it is very largely, though by no means exclusively, in the stocks and bonds of corporations that business gambling is carried on. I proceed to speak of certain other forms of uneconomic and unjust procedure which arise in connection with corporations.

Among the worst of these is the habit of forming from powerful members of main corporations sub-corporations, and turning over to these all the profits earned by the larger concerns. Several influential directors of a railroad corporation, for instance, may form themselves into a transportation company. The railway earns millions, and people wonder that it is so poor. Its stock yields no dividends and becomes valueless. At last a receiver is appointed, and the bondholders take the property, not seldom to be themselves wrecked in the same way in their turn.

Such a history has been passed through by so many railway properties in this country that it is almost the fashion. Mr. Edward Atkinson loves to boast how cheaply we can transport wheat from the West to the seaboard. The fact is that as a nation we are donating wheat and beef to England on a colossal scale each year. The present owners of railways can afford to transport for these small sums per ton-mile, but their facilities for doing this have cost the country as such a sum for which these minimal freight rates form no adequate return. By sub-incorporation, wrecking, and kindred processes, the first owners have been dispossessed in order that the new owners, paying next to nothing for the properties, may feed England for naught.

Another style of vicious obliquity in this field consists of multiplying the number of shares which represent a corporation's property, so that its face value is out of all proportion to the real value of the property represented. Corporate property, of course, often really expands in value, so that the stock representing it deserves to be increased. These cases of legitimate expansion suggest and make easier others which are not warranted. Sometimes the purpose of stock-watering is to get the money which the new stock will bring, the public being willing to pay high for it after the plant has had a spurt of specially high earnings, with too little regard for its permanent earning power. Oftener the purpose is to deceive public and employés. Profits as reckoned on stock valuation may be but three or four per cent., when, based on the cost or proper valuation of the plant, they would be treble or quadruple that. The lower rate of profit is always the one published, if any, so that competitors may not multiply, and employés may not clamor for higher wages.

Another iniquity to which corporations at times resort

is the freezing out of feeble stockholders by the strong ones. The method is to vote large repairs, making the property all the time more valuable, but dropping dividends. The poorer corporators need income, and sell their stock for what it will bring. The rich ones buy, at low figures, of course. When nearly all is in hand, dividends are declared again, the stock rises, and the plethoric holders sell, if they wish, at a huge advance.

After all, the worst trouble with great corporations is that, in a very true sense, they have no souls. Such a body must needs be administered, at bottom, by a salaried official, whose reward and reputation depend on the dividends won under his management. Such a functionary, to be truly human toward his employés, must be more than human. Every consideration prompts him to save wherever possible. As a lessening of wages is the readiest way to economize on any large scale, so often as he dares, or has any hope of succeeding, he is apt to try that. If taxed with hardness of heart, he says, — and his situation permits him to be quite conscientious in this — I must guard the interests of stockholders, many of whom are widows and orphans, needing the best dividends they can get. I must reduce wages; at any rate, I cannot raise them.

Meantime the actual employers, the stockholders, know nothing of their help. Employés never see ultimate employers; they rarely know who their employers are. They have to do only with the stern man at the office, to whom, too often, they are of no account save as instruments of gain for the concern.

That under such circumstance workingmen combine is surely no wonder. The miracle is that their solidarity is not more complete.

In the remainder of this lecture I raise the question how far, if at all, the system of industry going on about us works out justice between man and man. How perfectly is the industrial world an arena of righteousness? Can we trust industrial society, running automatically, as at present it, for the most part, does, to bring to each of the individuals composing it substantial fair play and equity? Ought our effort touching agitators and reformers to be to point them to the right path and to render them wise, or ought they to be squarely snubbed, and, if possible, repressed? I inquire, in fine, whether the God-fearing citizen, who wishes to work righteousness and see it wrought all about him, ought to be satisfied with our existing system, in the main, seeking only casual amendments here and there, or whether he ought to be on the outlook for considerably radical changes in it, and, when it can be clearly seen what alterations of that sort will be for the best, work for the introduction of such?

Not one of the great masters of English economics — Adam Smith, Ricardo, J. S. Mill, Cairnes, Jevons — has ever maintained that a perfectly automatic economic system would be perfectly just. It was reserved for Bastiat to turn automatic economics into a theodicy — to maintain that the free pursuit by each human being of his own welfare, as conceived by him, would result in the highest possible good of the community as a whole.

False as this tenet this, nothing can be more interesting than the reasoning which led to it. Its later devotees have felt called upon to square the economic order advocated by them with moral law, to justify it before the bar of moral reason. Bastiat went so far as to deny the doctrine of rent, because, if true, it would be unjust, breaking in upon his beautiful system of economic harmonies. Our American teachers who pretend to stand up for the economic faith as delivered by Adam Smith nearly all go beyond him to the position of Bastiat, proclaiming the state of affairs produced by perfect liberty to be the one wherein dwelleth righteousness.

It is necessary to appeal from them to Adam Smith, Ricardo, and Mill. I deny that the *laissez-faire* order is necessarily just or moral, or that it is best calculated to promote either the aggregation or the distribution of wealth. Industrial liberty has been, and still is, a mighty engine of good. The point is to work it, not to worship it; to take it, where we can, as an economic maxim, but not as imperative or sacred law even in economics, still less in morals.

There is special light in all this upon the most vexing question at present up in economic theory — that of distribution. All our darkness in this field, which is very dense, comes from the assumption that when we have found how economic causes within man and outside, acting independently of society's reason and volition, would distribute wealth if left to themselves, the result ought to be for the best good of all, and so to accord with righteousness. When the outcome is seen not to be of this character, most economists divide into two classes — those who wrest morals to suit their economics, and those who wrest economics to suit their morals. But why assume that automatic distribution must be of a moral cast or bring about the greatest good? It is hard to see why the operation of laws and forces in our nature and the universe, when not guided by reason, should partake of an ethical character any more in the economic realm than in the physical realm. If an earthquake knocks down your house, leaving you so much poorer — perhaps with nothing — you do not express surprise at the unethical character of the physical laws operative in the event. Why should you any more when poverty befalls you by the blind working of an economic law?

It seems to me that in automatic or unregulated economic distribution no ethical principle is to be found. If we unfortunately insist on naming automatic distribution "natural," then the same is to be said of "natural distribution," and we may as well end the quest for harmony between the ethical and the economic. Ungoverned, unguided, mechanical distribution will never be sure to issue in justice.

Of course, what agitators say has to be sifted. Poverty is not necessarily an evil; it may be deserved. Even if laziness is sometimes constitutional, unless it can be shown that the constitution has derived its perverse bent from social mal-adjustments, suffering through such laziness may be, sociologically considered, not an evil at all, but of remedial tendency, and, therefore, a good instead.

Nor is it a proper complaint that some are better off than others. They may have wrought or economized better. We feel as by a sort of intuition that gain gotten by the honest, open use of one's own powers, without artificial or accidental advantage of any kind, is earned; that it belongs to the possessor, so that no other has any right to view his possession as a hardship. That the gain has risen through superior native endowment no unprejudiced mind would regard as impairing the title, unless this has worked its victory through craft and cunning. It is only accidental or artificial advantages to which our moral sense objects.

We reach solid ground for complaint in the fact that the products of society's toil are not distributed to individuals according to the causality of individuals in creating these products. This is nearly the same as saying that many men are rich either altogether without economic merit, or wholly out of proportion to their economic merit. By economic merit is meant the quality which attaches to any human action or line of action in virtue of its advantageousness, on the whole and in the long run, to the material weal of the community. It assumes three forms. A man may claim economic merit when and so far as he is a wage-earner in any useful calling; when and so far as he earns economic profits, *i. e.*, secures profits by effort and agency of a genuinely economic kind, without trick, theft, monopoly, or any artificial advantage; and when and so far as he owns capital as distinguished from unproductive wealth. Capital is productive wealth; hence, a holder of capital must be indirectly, at any rate, a wealth-user. Such a functionary is called economically meritorious at this point, not as a final judgment or to beg the question against socialists, but provisionally, for the sake of argument. One could, doubtless, grant that this is a lower form of merit than would be realized were the holder also a worker; yet in society as at present organized, the mere holder of capital must be regarded as deserving well. We see this instantly if we suppose owners of capital to consume it instead of retaining it. We waive for the moment the question whether private capital is, on the whole, administered as well, as truly for society's good, as if society owned and administered it all, although the difference is certainly smaller than socialists contend.

These, then — wages-earning, profits-earning, and interest-earning — are the three forms of economic merit; but it goes almost without saying that wealth comes to many who are not meritorious in any of these ways, and to many others out of all proportion to such merit as they may have.

Through rise and fall in money values, through mere luck, through monopoly, through theft, and through gambling, it comes to pass that, under our present economic practice, one section of society eats, drinks,

Economic Evils due to Social Conditions 83

and is merry, to a greater or less extent, at the expense of the rest.

On the other hand, a great many men are poor without the slightest economic demerit. They are people who do the best they can, and always have done so. They are not dissipated, indolent, thriftless, or prodigal of children, but quite free from these vices, being in every way exemplary citizens and worthy members of the community. Yet they are poor, often very poor, never free from fear of want, doomed for life to the alternative of hard labor or starvation, and as thoroughly cut off from all means of culture proper, as completely precluded from the rational living of life, as were the Helots of old Sparta. Such human beings are to be found in every city of the world. They are less numerous in America than in Europe, but America has them, too. Let him who doubts read Mrs. Helen Campbell's *Prisoners of Poverty*, or, better, go among these poor people, converse with them, and judge for himself.

It has been carefully computed that in representative districts of East London no less than 55 per cent. of the very poor, and fully 68 per cent. of the other poor, are so because of deficiency of employment, while only 4 per cent. of the very poor and none of the other poor are loafers. It is estimated that 53 per cent. of the needy in New York City suffer for work instead of aid, and the willing idlers among these are certainly no more proportionally than in London. According to the Massachusetts Labor Statistics for 1887, almost a third of the people returned as usually engaged in remunerative toil were unemployed during nearly a third of the census year 1885. The working people of the State as a whole, averaged to be employed at their main occupations less than eleven months of the year. These results are not far from normal for this country, while for most others they are much too good to be normal. It must be admitted that the extreme division of labor has wrought its curse as well as its blessing. According to the Massachusetts statistics, only about one in eighteen of those deprived of their usual employment turned to another.

But is not the condition of the poor continually improving? Yes and no. Undoubtedly the average wage-worker can earn more pounds of wheat, meat, and coal, and more yards of cloth by twelve hours' work to-day than fifty years ago — probably enough more to make up for the greater unsteadiness of labor now. Mr. Giffen's statistics for England are well known. In the industries figured upon by him, nominal wages, making no allowance for lost time, have advanced since 1820-25 between 10 and 160 per cent. The average may be about 50 per cent. For this country the improvement is at least no less; I doubt if it is greater. Mr. Edward Atkinson's roseate pictures of laborers' progress are familiar to all. The French savant, M. Chevallier, has surveyed, as best he could, the whole industrial world, and is very sure that the laborer's prosperity has advanced everywhere.

I incline to think that materially the workingman is

gaining a little, though, when the modern uncertainty of labor is considered, the improvement is comparatively slight. Many representations, as commonly pressed and understood, gravely mislead. Thus when Mr. Goschen, a few years ago, showed that the number of small fortunes and incomes in England was increasing faster than large, faster than fortunes in general, faster than population, he did not touch the really poor at all. He dealt with incomes of $750 and upwards per year, estates under $5,000 in value, house rents of $100 and on, small shareholdings, small insurance policies, and the like. But what is all this to the caravans of poor fellows with starvation incomes, or none at all? Is it not almost mockery to argue hope from a more felicitous distribution of "estates," "rents," "policies," and "shares" in Britain, when English villages, unable to give employment, are emptying their impoverished sons and daughters into the cities at the rate of 60,000 or 70,000 yearly, only to make their situation, if possible, worse yet; when the sweating system is forcing men and women to work sometimes for 33 and even 36 consecutive hours to avoid starvation; and when the hungry hordes of East London poor, but for the Christian work done among them, or for fear of the police, would speedily march to the sack of the West End!

The common statement about wages as increasing faster than income from invested wealth neither has, nor can have, statistical proof, because we have no public, or even private, registry of profits. So, too, the apparent fact that a greater and greater proportion of the nation's product goes year by year as wages does not necessarily imply a rising rate of wages, but may accompany falling wages; and it will do so if population increases faster than the wages fund. And when wages-statistics are adduced to show improvement, nothing can exceed the recklessness with which they are sometimes made and handled. Wages of superintendence frequently swells the apparent average. Account is rarely taken of shut-downs and slack work, or of those unable to find work at all.

In many respects, indeed, the toiling masses are no whit better off to-day than in England four centuries ago. The late Thorold Rogers, describing the Plantagenet and Tudor age, declares that then "there were none of those extremes of poverty and wealth which have excited the astonishment of philanthropists, and are now exciting the indignation of workmen. . . Of poverty which perishes unheeded, of a willingness to do honest work and a lack of opportunity, there was little or none."

The fact is that, while the poor man has been getting on, he has not retained his old-time closeness to the average weal. Let us take a rubber strap, fasten one end, and extend the other till the length is doubled. If now we note the changes in the relative positions of points between the middle and the fixed extremity, we shall find that each, though further from the end than before, is also further from the middle; that, besides, the points nearest the end have moved least, those nearest the middle most. Of those between the middle and the free end, all are now further beyond the middle than before, while each has gained the more the remoter it was at first.

Much in this way has society stretched out in the matter of economic welfare. There at the fixed point of dire poverty stand the masses, as they have always stood. Our heaping up of wealth, Pelion upon Ossa, elevates them no iota. Their neighbors have removed from the dead point a little, but the center has gone away from them still more. Those nearer the average at first, and still beneath it, have drifted further from the fixed extreme, but not one among them is so close to the middle as he began. Only when you pass beyond the average do you come to men who have gained upon the average, and these have accomplished this in proportion to the advantage which they had at the start.

While the poor man should be very glad that his toil brings him more and better food, raiment, and shelter than once, the fact that it does so is no sign that his condition is improved in the sense in which this expression is usually understood. Richer supply for one's mere bodily wants does not signify that one is getting forward, or even holding one's own, in humanity's general advance. Let man as a race remove further and further from the condition of brutes, and let me in the meantime keep as near to the average of human weal as ever — that is what I want. So long as I am falling behind the average comfort, welfare, culture, intelligence, and power, it insults my manhood to remind me that my sweat commands per drop a little more bread. "It is written, man shall not live by bread alone." And in this higher life, the only one in respect to which it is really worth while to discuss the question at length, hosts of men in civilized countries are making no progress whatever, but are relatively losing ground.

It is amazing to hear bright thinkers arguing as if poverty were always due to the fault of the people who suffer it, as if there were some providence or natural law which would make it impossible for one man ever to smart for the misdeeds of another. Not seldom this is exactly what occurs. In fact, one of the very worst vices of present industry is that it continually visits curses upon men for results which they had not the slightest hand in originating. It is said that profits are justifiable because the employer takes risks — a position entirely just so long as the present system prevails. But it is not the profit-maker alone who is involved in the risks he takes. His help are bound up with him; and, if he proves to be rash, while he himself will only have to surrender this or that luxury, they may starve or freeze. When over-production, again, either alone or aided by over-speculation, or by those changes in the value of money referred to in the last lecture, has evoked a commercial crisis, the poor, who have had nothing whatever to do with causing it, are the chief sufferers.

How slight is even the economic betterment usually

alleged, compared with what, from foreknowledge of the character of the age, one would have been justified in anticipating! Such progress in all the industrial arts, such cheapening of wares, such opening of new continents in North and South America, and in Africa and Australia, the richest in bread-yield and beef-yield of any beneath the sun, should, it would seem, have annihilated poverty. Yet the amelioration is only well perceptible for wage-workers as a class, and for the unskilled it is hardly this. Still less can any general law of economic progress, covering the centuries, be established. On the contrary, the passing of this age of industrial advance and of world-wide land utilization with so slight gain in the ordinary comforts of life on the part of the laboring man, goes far to preclude all hope of great improvement for him under present economic conditions.

We began this lecture by analyzing the iniquity of business gambling. That led us to consider corporations, and the numerous ways in which men are wronged through their operations. Enlarging our view, we then surveyed the general question how far equity results from the working of the economic system as now guided and inspired. This study has led to the conclusion that society must yet develop a good way, evolve new regulations and methods, or somehow receive new inspiration and guidance, before ours will be an earth wherein righteousness shall dwell.

I conclude with three remarks :

1. The evils contemplated are none the less evils even if no way of overcoming them should ever be discovered.

2. Few of the wrongs brought to light involve personal guilt or sin on any one's part. They mainly consist of social maladjustments, for which no one in particular is responsible, and which are to be removed, if at all, by general social effort.

3. The outlook may be less dark than it now seems. Sociology is a new and callow science. Let the hard study which the last two generations have bestowed on Physical Science be applied for the next two generations to Social Science, and the result may be, if not heaven, at least a tolerable earth.

V
SOCIALISM

FOR the wrongs and distresses remarked upon in the preceding lectures a remedy is announced that many regard sure, easy, and final. It is Socialism. Socialism has, now-a-days, too many, too honest, and too thoughtful devotees to be ignored. It is old enough, too, to demand a measure of regard on the score of age. It is stronger at this moment than ever before, and is rapidly growing. Conservative teachers and students are, indeed, forced to scan the claims of this loud pretender, because of his energetic and successful propaganda among the masses. Hardly a northern State is without its socialist press. Marx is translated and widely read, his foremost theses serving as texts on a thousand socialist platforms every Sunday. Besides, however the subject may repel us, if we only study it with candor and thoroughness, it cannot but instruct us as well.

Socialism is a hard term to define, so protean is the thing which it names, so loose the speech of writers. In a sense, every man is a socialist who believes that the automatic way of distributing the rewards of industry inevitably works injustice, and that therefore righteousness in distribution lies along some other path.

But this definition includes, among others, communists, who wish enjoyment and possession in common as well as production in common, and also anarchists, whose favorite idea is that government, as distinguished from administration, can be and ought to be abolished. From both these groups proper socialists justly demand to be kept apart. As opposed to the communist, the real socialist does not expect or desire complete leveling in social place or in economic condition. As contrasted with the anarchist, he believes in continuing some form of real political power.

Although socialist ideas have agitated every civilized century, Socialism as we know it to-day arrived only with Karl Marx (1818–1883) and Karl Rodbertus (1805–1875), two German thinkers whose reasonings have stirred the economic world. Their views are at bottom much alike, yet not exactly. One mastering Rodbertus masters Marx; but you may grasp and refute Marx, leaving many of Rodbertus's positions unshaken and unappreciated. Rodbertus has presented Socialism in by far its most engaging and persuasive form, free, in his intention at any rate, from nearly all those extravagant and offensive traits which disfigure other expositions. But Marx is the more severely logical, the more uncompromising, and far the more popular among such as would welcome almost any radical change in the existing order of things.

Marx's and Rodbertus's form of Socialism, with which I shall mainly deal — classical Socialism, that is — is the form which arouses the most enthusiasm on the part of theorists. Marx's writings are its scriptures. It is at the basis of all the socialist strivings on the European continent, and also in America. Being the standard quality of the thing, I pay it the most attention.

In England, however, has developed, within recent years, a milder form of Socialism, less theoretical, less thorough, which has attracted to itself a very large number of sincere and temperate adherents, men who are not cranks at all. I refer to the Socialism of the Fabian Society. Stringent Socialism believes, first, that the economic condition of a State determines absolutely its intellectual, moral, social, and religious development; second, that automatic industry inevitably begets an iniquitous surplus value, which laborers create but their employers enjoy; and third, that all productive operations and property, without exception, should be in the hands of the State. The Fabians, on the contrary, deny every one of these propositions. They are not of opinion that the economic state of a people is the sole determinant of its entire weal; they do not believe in Marx's doctrine of an inevitable surplus value in private industry; and they do not insist that all productive processes without exception shall be taken over from private into public control. At the end of the lecture, I shall have something further to say about this type of Socialism. Meantime let us try to understand Socialism proper.

Not a few pretty well read people, when Socialism is mentioned, call to mind Babœuf with his bedlam, Fourier with his phalansteries, or at least Louis Blanc and his public factories, construing the system through conceptions of rigid force, tyranny, or military discipline. Others know Socialism to be a contemporary phenomenon, yet conceive Lassalle, Bebel, Liebknecht, or the Zürich *"Social-demokrat"* to be its sole or best representative. Were any such mistaken notion correct, the system would be unworthy of serious thought. Personal liberty and the opportunity for untrammeled individual development are the best products of civilization. Any proposition toward social change which jeopardizes these will, and deservedly, sink of its own weight, however much promise of mere animal comfort it may have to recommend it. On this, Rodbertus and Marx would speak as strongly as Professor Sumner.

Both strenuously insist that their system would permit every man to choose his calling as freely as now; to follow his peculiar bent, his preferred beliefs, religious and other; to save up titles to wealth for his support in old age, or to bequeath to those closely related to him; to buy books and works of art; to do deeds of charity; to travel abroad. They maintain, indeed, that while the present method of industry only permits these sweet liberties to a select few, theirs would throw them open to all who were diligent and thrifty. Whether or not they herein judge their theory justly, we shall see later.

Rodbertus, although he misplaces and mis-expounds

intellectual labor, does not ignore it, as nearly all the other socialists persistently do. He is fully aware that an army of laborers needs its officers as well as an army of soldiers, and that in both cases the so indispensable exertion of brain power must be duly rewarded.*

All the socialists make much of the state, the public power, having authority over every citizen.

It is here that anarchists and socialists divide. The strictly economic tenets of the two parties are identical. Both restrict the legitimate range of private property to that wealth which, like food, clothing, houses, books, and similar personal belongings, has no other destination but to be consumed, making it the business of society in general to administer both the great instrumentalities of production, land and capital. They agree in repudiating as an accursed thing the entire *laissez-faire* belief. The system of free competition, both say, never brings with it fair competition, but is instead a ruthless war of strong with weak. It is wasteful, they further affirm, through lack of coördination in industry and through failure neatly to adjust supply and demand; and it continually lets vast amounts of land and capital lie idle, because this is cheaper for the owners, murderous as it is for society.

And the two philosophies are at one in assuming that the public conduct of productive industry would remedy these evils. The thought is that an indefinitely more copious production would thus result, making it safe

---
* On Rodbertus's Socialism, see my article in the *Journal of Polit. Econ.*, Vol. 1, No. 1.

heavily to bond the country, if necessary, to pay off present proprietors. The improvement is expected to come in part from a more perfect organization of industry, saving waste of labor and of capital, but mainly from the fresh hope and courage which would inspire the laboring masses. All willing to work might have work. Thirst for inordinate wealth would cease. Every hour's toil would be paid for at its true worth, no deduction being made to pamper the lazy capitalist in his useless life. Through a system of labor-time-money, each commodity or service would be purchasable at its precise cost in labor. Society would no longer be robbed by gambling in stocks or produce, or industry palsied by fluctuations in the value of money. Commercial crises would be unknown, while, corporations being no longer possible, their threat to just government, along with the frauds of their managers, would have passed away for ever.

Rodbertus was, I think, the first to point out, what now nearly every student of the subject admits, that the existing order of economic society inevitably encounters commercial panics at frequent intervals. A period of prosperous production has place, wages are good, and products of all sorts are multiplied. By and by, wares do not sell well, and the manufacturers wonder. The explanation is perfectly simple. The hand-workers, naturally constituting the great mass of the consumers, cannot continue to purchase freely because the inequitable distribution which the present system involves is continually lessening their share of the total social product. Want is thus prevented from becoming effective demand. The crisis is a rough method of redressing the unequal distribution, by getting goods into the hands of the poor at less than cost. When, at excruciating pain to all, this process has been achieved, the wheels of industry start anew, only, however, to become clogged again in due time, by the same causes as before.

Other crying vices of economic life as now regulated, the socialists, like other people, clearly see,— riches without merit, poverty without demerit, men forced to serve men, cross purposes in production, inducing infinite waste and injustice, idle wealth that might be aiding industry but is not, fraud in trade and manufacture, and the tyranny and menace of corporate power.

Socialism proposes a regimen for the correction of this terrible depravity in our economic relations. Its ideas are few and simple, but sweeping. Practically they reduce to two.

One is that the state shall own and administer, as the sole and universal *entrepreneur*, both the essential helps to human production, viz., land and capital proper. The last, capital proper, means all wealth whose sole destiny is to increase wealth, such as mills, machinery and tools, means of transportation, warehouses, stores, and the like. On the other hand, wealth destined for personal use, as clothing, books, works of art, horses, carriages, and probably dwellings, though produced by the state, could be purchased and be subject to private ownership. Of such things every citizen would be free to possess all that his industry and thrift would bring him, and to make use of it as he pleased, without let or hindrance from any one.

The other proposition is, that all labor of every kind is to be paid for in labor-time-money, or certificates of labor, and the prices of all things fixed and stated in terms and denominations of the same medium.

In issuing these certificates to pay labor, the hour or day of ordinary, unskilled labor is to be taken as the unit, and all forms of skilled labor to be reduced to a common denominator with this, by accurately ascertaining the time and cost required to master those higher forms. Thus, while the street-sweeper or the shoveler would get a unit of the time-money for his day's work, the journeyman watchmaker would get, perhaps, four for his, the master watchmaker seven or eight, and so on. All money and all wages or salaries is to consist of tickets representing so many hours or days of simple labor.

To correspond with this, each product of labor is to be stamped, by means of similar tickets, with the number of hours spent in its production, the skilled labor, if any, being reduced to its equivalent amount of simple labor.

Suppose the whole community-day's work to embrace nine million individual-day's works of six hours each, unequal quality and intensity being reduced to simple labor time. Then the whole daily product will be equivalent to six community-hours of work, or to fifty-four million individual-hours of work. If the daily demand for public purposes averaged one-third of the product of a community-day's work, a very liberal estimate, there would remain as goods to be consumed each day by individuals, the equivalent in cost of four community, or thirty-six million individual, labor hours.

Provided the kinds and groups of goods composing the part of the national product consumable by individuals could be made, through precise statistics and practical equalization from the public reserves, to correspond exactly to the kinds and groups of individual demands, then one could calculate exactly what part or multiple of a single average day's work each portion of every kind of goods ought to exchange for, so as to attach the proper label. A man's orders upon the various forms of goods desired and accessible could cover at least two-thirds of the product of his normal day's work of six hours. In fact, products left behind by deceased people, with gifts from the public-spirited, would probably cover so much of the public need that each citizen could, as a rule, consume nearly all that he created.

You work. Your pay consists in an amount of labor-time-tickets precisely answering to the number of hours you have wrought, reduced to the simple labor hour scale. Wishing to purchase, you are given, at any of the state's bazaars, wares whose cost in labor-time, as stamped on them, precisely equals the labor-time which it took you to earn the tickets given in payment. "To every man according as his work shall be."

See what, according to socialists' expectation, follows

from the realization of these two ideas,— state industry and labor-time money.

1. Crises come no more. There is just enough production in each line to answer the demand, as revealed by careful statistics; while, since workers get their full share of the profits, want in every case becomes effective demand, so that no stock is left over. No shops or machinery rot unused. The New York Central Railway no longer hauls San Francisco freight from Rochester, first to New York, and then straight back through Rochester again. Fatal competition of railway with railway and of shop with shop is abolished for ever.

2. Every one who will work has work, and at an absolutely fair and equitable wage, out of which nothing is kept back to pamper any one in idleness; yet no one in order to secure work has to duck or subject himself to his fellow-man.

3. Corporations exist no longer, since there is no place or business for them, the state producing everything which anyone can ask. Also, corporations gone, stocks, the stock market and the whole blood-sucking activity attaching thereto, is entirely banished. Business gambling in all its forms is made impossible.

4. Money, as known to history, has given way to a substitute far its superior. Its fluctuations in value, with the silent blight they used to shed abroad, no longer afflict. Gold and silver may all be used in the arts. If their cheapness disgusts people with them, far less will be produced, and so much toil will be set free for things more useful.

5. The full benefit of monopolies and of production on a gigantic scale will be realized, and will contribute, not to feed and foster a small band of *bourgeoisie* barons, but to enrich and exalt to a rational life the entire community of us now in vain struggling to rise.

We have thus set forth the socialist's diagnosis of society's economic disease, and his proposal for a cure. Both have been described fairly, and indeed sympathetically rather than the reverse. How far, now, can we agree with the teachings that we have been examining?

Most of us would probably go a good way toward acquiescence in this account of men's economic distress. Altogether valuable as well as grave is the truth the socialist tells us in that regard. But when he proposes for the cure that thoroughgoing scheme of state undertakings, we make a long pause. Many pause and do no more; or, if they speak, it is only to curse and swear. That is not right. Wise are the words of Schæffle: "You have not refuted a practical thought when you have sketched no plan whatever by which it might conceivably be carried out, or even drawn a caricature of such. Fairly to judge ideas of this sort, having a practical aim, you must set to work by supposing the most reasonable scheme for their execution which you can think of."

Public ownership of land and capital is of course quite conceivable. Already, here as in every other civilized country, the state is the greatest single owner of both capital and land, and the most extensive single employer of labor. If necessary, it may extend its economic sphere.

But such state contractorship would avail nothing of consequence apart from the institution of labor-time-money and labels to fix wages by desert and the prices of things by their cost ; and about this scheme a thousand insurmountable difficulties gather.

Communism can be instituted and carried on without any such device as this, which, probably, is a leading reason why Communism tends almost everywhere to supplant scientific Socialism. When both were alive, Marx had the victory over Bakunin, who then captained the Communist hosts ; but now, I believe, Bakuninists grow more rapidly than Marxists. Mr. Bellamy's book *Looking Backward* is communist, not socialist. His policy is to divide the yearly product between the men, women, and children over a certain age, making up society, quite regardless of their respective efforts and contributions in production. That is a most easy programme. Such as think that it can be made to work with present or even prospective human nature, are enthusiastic for its introduction. But the genuine socialist does not, any more than the rest of us, wish an equal division of unequal earnings, and he is, therefore, obliged to devise some sort of a calculus by which social co-operation may be carried out, with its admitted and tremendous advantages, and yet every producer receive a reward proportioned to his share in the production, neither cheating any nor being cheated by any.

The Fabians, and most socialists in this country, have

not, I am sure, sufficiently considered this difficulty. The system would, no doubt, have to be dubbed Socialism were we merely to constitute the state our universal landlord and business manager, making no effort to r gulate the rewards of different classes of laborers or to fix the prices of products. But every one must see that if this alone is done, competition of man with man remains almost as now, while fluctuations in money, the same as now, will continue a source of the rankest injustice. If nothing more radical than that is involved in Socialism, the cause is not worth agitation.

The great socialists have, therefore, been bent on a plan for exactly determining costs of things and rewards of services; and, as I have said, any such scheme is beset with a thousand difficulties.

I do not count as chief among these the problem of reducing the different forms of activity usually recognized as labor, to hours of common labor, because, the system being once launched, any kind of ordinary toil at first estimated too low would be deserted, as any appraised too high would be sought by crowds and overdone.

Another step, however, brings us to utter perplexity. While labor is the main cause of value, there are various other causes, so that the amount of labor in a commodity is almost never, and never with certainty, a measure of its value. Further, even were labor a perfect gauge of value in every case, it is impossible to estimate, with any accuracy, the amount of labor stored up in any given article. You cannot find out how much labor is represented in a thing, and if you could, that labor would not with any exactness exhibit its value. These facts make the socialist's scheme quite unworkable, or at least so complex and hard of application, as to render fatuous all hope from it of greater equity in distribution than now exists.

The labor of public officers, of teachers, and of men engaged in useful scientific pursuits, enters into every manufactured commodity, but intangibly and very unequally. Still, if you wish to allow for it, to increase the price of a brick, say, to help liquidate the chief justice's salary, there is no other way than to lump his salary with all expenses of that order, and to distribute the resultant sum over bricks and other products according to their cost apart from these peculiar general expenses. Such distribution could not be effected with more than the roughest approach to fairness.

This is perhaps why Rodbertus does not pretend to reckon governmental expenses, and the like, or even salaries for superintendence or the remuneration of any form of intellectual work, into the cost of producing wares, and why he identifies labor with material labor. But he does not thus evade the difficulty, since he is forced to institute a system of taxation to meet those general outlays, and the assessment of the tax would involve the very same inequity as the distribution of the cost just referred to.

Again, the labor of a painter or sculptor, of an architect, of an orator, of a singer, of a skilled physician or surgeon, is material labor — labor, therefore, in Rodbertus's sense; but how can such kinds of exertion be reduced to a time scale? Who, for instance, will undertake to measure in hours of simple labor one hour's work of that great contemporary surgeon who has performed ovariotomy one hundred and twenty-five times in succession without the loss of a life?*

Again, suppose that a laborer has been receiving for a given amount of work ten hours of labor-time money, but that after some months the numbers crowding into his trade make it clear that nine hours was his proper wage. He is accordingly cut down to nine hours. Is the state at the same time to lower the labor price of that product ten per cent., that is, from ten hours to nine? Manifestly not, for that were to throw away what was unsold at the time of the reduction. The price would have to be reduced gradually from ten hours to nine; but every one who has purchased before that figure is reached, will have been, by socialist principles, cheated, having been forced to pay for his ware more than its labor-cost. The same occurs if a ware has been costing a hundred hours of labor time, and a new machine is invented which reduces this number to fifty. The price must be lowered gradually or the old stock will be wasted.

Again, there are certain desirable goods which cannot be placed in the market every day in quantities just sufficient to supply all who want them. Potatoes may rot between two harvests. In agriculture, no art will ever be able to equate supply and demand exactly.

---

* Dr. Thomas Keith, of Edinburg.

During the snow blockade of March, 1888, milk sold in New York City one day for five and six dollars per can of forty quarts, and the second day after for a dollar. There is hardly one product which may not at times thus have to be offered at a scarcity-price instead of its cost-price. If the price in such a case is simply the labor cost, only the first comers after the turning out of each new batch can be served, the rest going entirely destitute. Were the commodity bread-corn, they would starve to death. Such "getting left" would be as bad as old *laissez-faire* privations, not to be tolerated. But there would be no means of avoiding it except to raise the price, and find out who wanted such articles most — departing, that is, from cost price and so from socialist principles.

Again, there are very many articles, like wine, wood, and timber, which, after their production proper, take on value by simple lapse of time. Socialist theory requires us to sell old wine at practically the same cost as new; seasoned timber as low as green timber. But if we do so, depend upon it, lame and asthmatic people will never get any old wine or seasoned woods, all being taken before they arrive. Such things, too, must not be sold at prices which accord with their cost, but at prices according with the demand for them.

Also, in spite of the best possible management, there will be shop-worn goods, goods left over from the old year, and goods out of taste as to style; an enormous class in all, which must either be thrown away or disposed of according to demand, at far less than cost.

Again, the productivity of a nation's labor varies with periods. Now the prices of wares for the current period, if the rule is followed, must of course be fixed according to their labor-cost in some preceding period. In all likelihood, therefore, it will never happen that labor will be exactly remunerated, according to the theory, and the dissidence must often be immense. The only way to mollify this evil, which can never be entirely removed, will be to price nearly every class of goods now higher, now lower than their cost.

This fault of the theory is wholly independent of the preceding ones. It would, of course, sometimes more or less offset the others; sometimes it would aggravate them.

This criticism suggests another, namely, that in the long run, as production is cheapened, labor tickets that have been some months outstanding, increase in purchasing power. Two results follow from this, both significant: first, the utter impossibility of labeling goods in agreement with the costs of all tickets, old and new, that purchasers may offer; and, second, the encouragement of hoarding, which is contrary to the entire genius of Socialism.

The tickets, we well know, under Socialism are not to be permitted to draw interest. How, unless through punitory statute, loaning at interest will be prevented by Socialism, I for my part could never see. The system certainly admits of it. It must be intended to make borrowing or lending a crime.

Again, the demand for a given class of goods, and

also the pressure into a given avenue of labor, will vary with the years, and it may thus come to pass that a given sort of work grows popular just as the demand for its products falls off. The state must either lower the wages for such industry, raising them when the reverse conditions prevail, or else assume the tyrannical office of forcing citizens into and out of employments like so many cattle.

One cannot help mentioning it as another count against the plan of society here under review, that by it all foreign trade would probably have to be excluded in order to keep goods from being sold at less than state cost at home. Imports would, of course, throw the domestic supply and demand into confusion, and hence be inadmissible. But the restriction thus rendered necessary could not but entail needless cost in production, besides greatly hindering in its march the world's civilization. The alternative to exclusion would be foreign trade under state regulation, but there is no way by which the cost of imports in domestic labor-time could be kept the same for any number of weeks.

We have thus discovered, it would seem, that the effort to make cost the exact rule of price must fail. The plan criticised would, it is believed, leave the gap between prices and costs fully as great on the whole as it is under free competition; while it would secure this far approach between prices and costs only by constant artificial tinkering with price-lists, which would at best be costly, and would keep the public authorities under perpetual suspicion of jobbery.

This opens another difficulty. Suppose that the scheme were intrinsically feasible, and that we all have thus far urged to the contrary had to be unsaid; to succeed, such a social order as socialists wish would require in public servants not only almost preternatural skill, but also a stoical hardihood of integrity more difficult as yet to find than the philosopher's stone.

And it is impossible to suppose that the wonderful richness of invention and of enterprise and daring, mastering nature and bringing forth ever new devices for the comfort and elevation of mankind, would go on as now were the spurs of individual initiative and personal profit removed. The same criticism applies here, only in a much more emphatic way, which I made in the second lecture, touching the prevalence of business trusts and combinations. They endanger progress by discouraging industrial alertness. It is easy to reply that philanthropy will take the place of the incentive just named. It might do so were it certain to be forthcoming, but philanthropy is something which cannot be provided on simple notification. Give us the love of man in due degree, and we can work the present system successfully.

And the proletariat? You will read socialists' volumes in vain for any sufficing word telling how their system is after all to remedy unenforced poverty. There are hints. We learn, for instance, that so soon as it amounts to something to save and lay up and try to get on, all people will be thrifty. There is much in this thought; but there is not enough. Hope and even certainty of competence by work will not cure that deep, that total depravity of laziness which curses at least one per cent. even of our Saxon population. Go into any country town of New England. Look around, and you shall find middle-aged American men in rags, without a cent's worth of property or credit, who, but for this damnable economic vice, might be independently well off; without large families, rarely sick, and never having seen a day when they could not have earned fair wages if willing to work. What would Socialism boot such men? Nothing. Their need is a moral one. That, however, is a species of lack which no socialist ever properly recognizes.

Let the socialist deny it or disguise it as he will, his ordering of our economic life would certainly dull energy, repress personal initiative, and level humanity downward a good way while leveling it up, as it might, a little. The whole administration of Socialism must be a process of lumping and averaging, wherein the best men would be mulcted for doing their best and the poorest not mulcted for lagging behind and taking things easily. Socialists tell us that in their millenium no charity will be given. They cannot, however, mean to let the honest victims of accident or misfortune starve. For such there must be regular provision. And how will fraud upon the eleemosynary fund be prevented then more than now? There can be no mistake; the thrifty will continue to be the prey of the thriftless. Without an entire transformation of human nature, no system of Socialism yet devised offers any relief that cannot be had by other means; while any such resort must threaten evils the most dire and desperate.

Many of the strictures that have been made apply with less force, if at all, to Socialism of the Fabian stripe. In the Fabian programme a host of people could concur more or less fully, who could not accept at all the tenets or proposals of the thorough-going doctrine. However, Fabianism itself seems to me to be a good deal out of the way. As I have previously said in these lectures, I have no objection to increasing the function of the state when it is clearly seen to be desirable and at the same time safe. No doubt, moreover, much more must be expected of the state in the way of regulation, control, and out and out ownership, as the years pass. Is not this admission equivalent to the adoption of the Fabian policy?

Not at all. The Fabian says: "Let us place under state ownership all industry so far as the state can be made ready to operate it." The presupposition of this doctrine is in favor of state industry. I would take precisely the opposite ground. Let us retain the immense advantages of individual initiative, with the accompanying results of maximum enterprise and inventiveness, wherever such initiative is not erected into an abuse of society. Let us resort to state agency only when, and so far as, this is rendered necessary by the power and disposition on the part of individuals and private corporations to maltreat the public at large.

It may be said that a programme like this would in the end produce nearly the same results as Fabianism. I do not think so. It may indeed ultimately enlarge the sweep of state agency somewhere nearly as much as Fabianism would; but, should it do this, it will do it under the influence of the conservative and moderating thought that individualism, properly guarded, is precious, and that the state is not necessarily a worker of righteousness.

However, it is not clear that safety will ever require the public power to assume a very great number of industries. We have as yet hardly begun experiment in the direction of careful public regulation of massive industry. Let us press this. Let us enforce consideration for the interests of the people on the part of the mightiest industrial organizations. Progress in this will be slow. Yet great betterment in this line is clearly possible, while the socialist proposal, even in the modest form of the Fabian Society, sounds like moving the previous question on a motion to introduce the millenium.

We began this lecture by distinguishing Socialism proper from Communism and from Anarchism, and the thorough-going Socialism of Rodbertus and Marx from the timid programme of the Fabian Society. The proposals of thorough Socialism were then set forth, followed by a description of the socialist calculus, or means for securing the just, though unequal, distribution of products. The necessity of such a calculus was shown, whereon it was argued that no such calculus could be made to work in a way much to relieve the unfairness of the present system. Concluding, we recurred to Fabianism, the policy of progressive public ownership with incidental private industry, to which was opposed, as being deemed preferable, the policy of regulated private industry with incidental public ownership.

VI

WEAL AND CHARACTER

EVERY lecture in the course thus far has borne testimony to the intimate relation subsisting between human character and human welfare. Nearly all the woes of humanity to which our attention has been turned are due, directly or indirectly, to some moral difficulty. The curse of Adam would seem to be still in force, "in the sweat of thy face shalt thou eat thy bread." If men will depart from God, the happiness, even of a temporal order, which they might have enjoyed, becomes either impossible to them or attainable only through the utmost strife and pain. Could our race be duly developed morally, any one of several social schemes which now seem hardly more than chimeras might be made to work out happiest results.

The first lecture set forth two terrible vices, indolence and idle luxury, which are very prevalent among wealthy people. I see no possible way to the removal of these, or to their considerable amelioration, but by a change for the better in people's moral temper. The peculiar threat to society offered by combinations of capital, to wit, the loss of enterprise and of inventiveness, is certain to defy all other correctives but enlarged and intensified philanthropy.

What keeps up the world's vicious systems of land tenure, taxation, and money? It is at bottom naught else but men's selfishness, influential members or classes in society having, or thinking that they have, an interest in maintaining present abuses, and sturdily refusing to let justice be done. Nothing but the greed of a powerful creditor class in Great Britain hinders the immediate establishment in the world of a righteous and beneficent system of money, that would put an end to hard times for an indefinite term and perhaps for ever. Bad taxation and bad land laws are equally due to the selfishness of those benefited, or thought to be so, by the existing order. No doubt apathy and ignorance play a great part in conserving abuses in these fields, but such apathy and ignorance are themselves very largely due to selfishness.

To substantially the same cause must be ascribed the infelicities canvassed in Lecture IV: gambling, the criminal manipulation of corporations, and the various unfair advantages of some men over others. The form which part of these vices now take would perhaps disappear in consequence of certain mere mechanical changes that might occur in the structure of society; but the essence of them would outlast such changes and yield only to moral force.

The majority of us have read with pleasure Mr. Bellamy's book, "Looking Backward," and whatever other impressions it may have left upon us, this has doubtless remained, that society as at present constituted wastes a great deal of force in friction and cross purposes, which a system of socialism like Bellamy's might save. Every one will admit that were it safe for the state to carry on more industries, many that are now in private hands could be thus administered far more cheaply. The great trusts are proving how much less costly it is intrinsically to manufacture on a colossal scale. The state could of course do this on a more colossal scale than all the trusts together. Should any city in New England take marketing or gas lighting into its own hands, could it employ as keen talent, as masterful skill and enterprise as are now in use, it could pay all expenses and save one-third of the present cost to every consumer.

Why can we not, then, thus throw half or two-thirds of our industries into the state's hands? Simply because there is not at present character enough in the state's average *personnel*. Men are not good enough yet. We have desperate trouble to get honesty in public servants for the little work we ask of them now. Double or treble this work, double or treble the temptation for selfish men to press into official places, and society would literally break in pieces for corruption. On the other hand, let virtue multiply so that every public servant whom we elect can be trusted whatever we ask of him, and I do not say or believe that socialism will come, but I do say that many industries now in private hands will go over to the state, greatly to the easement and profit of us all.

It will be replied that there are good men enough for public offices, and for all the new offices that would be demanded were the state's authority never so much enlarged. Happily, this is true. There are good men enough, if we could only get them; but this fact does not diminish our woe, since public spirit is too feeble to seek out those citizens who are worthy of public places and to assure their election.

How much wealth is sunk, how much harder the conditions of life are made for nearly all, by the frauds and the thieving which are so prevalent in business circles: bank robberies, bank wrecking, and the gambling and other vicious practices to which we have adverted before! People wonder why it is, when our land is so rich and we work so hard, that there are so many poor, and that those of us who are not exactly poor are so constantly put to it to keep from being poor. The common answer is that poverty is the result of shiftlessness and drink. In part it is so, but by no means wholly. The cause is to a great extent this villainy in the business world, keeping men alive and in affluence who do little or nothing to increase the social store. This, in the main, is what renders the competition of life so hard. Capital might be cheaper, and wages higher in consequence, were dishonest men made honest.

It is the same in the labor world. Ask any intelligent head of a labor fraternity, a trade-union, a brotherhood, an assembly of the Knights of Labor, what the labor interest most needs, and he will tell you that it is "organization." "With proper organization," he will say, "laborers could do all things." He is right. With sufficiently solid organization labor would be the master of capital and could never become its slave. With proper organization, laborers could even enforce an eight-hour day. With organization, all wage-workers standing together, a universal strike for higher wages could be inaugurated and carried through, and considerably higher wages be obtained.

Why, then, do laborers not have better organization? Because men are too selfish. Labor organization on a broad scale demands character, good faith, honor, integrity. Now, as soon as any place of honor is created in a society or club formed for this purpose, bargains are made, rank selfishness manifests itself, and the result is that not the best man gets the office, but a second or third-rate man. Or, if it chances otherwise, and the most deserving fellow is elected, cliques are formed against him and he sooner or later falls a victim to the envy of his comrades. This is why labor organizations are usually such small and feeble bodies relatively to the whole number of laborers whom one would expect them to comprise. Moreover, they fight against one another. The Knights of Labor promised well for a time, but the order is at present much enfeebled by strifes within its membership.

These are evils which you cannot correct by legislation. The ablest and sharpest bank directors and bank examiners cannot prevent an adroit cashier from wrecking the bank and going to Canada if he is minded to do so. Laws are impotent to prevent gambling in stocks or upon the exchanges, or to make laboring men stand by one another. What we need in all these departments of society is a higher development of moral conviction — character, honesty, godliness. New York business men tell me that there is among them to-day a recognition of this in a higher demand for character on the part of responsible officials, a premium on rectitude and moral accomplishments. More surely than for many years, if a bank president or cashier is wanted, not the most brilliant man is selected, unless his integrity is also acknowledged, but the man who, being fairly versed in the business required, is most certain not to steal.

Just as thinkers have come to see that legislation is no cure-all, so most of them have concluded that the policy of social automatism or of leaving everything to the operation of what is called natural law, is no better. Herbert Spencer has been the great advocate of this evangel. His optimistic view of the way in which pure *laissez-faire* evolution is to regenerate our race and bring in the millenium is familiar to all. Both theory and facts oppose hope of progress in this manner. In his remarkable Romanes Lecture, at Oxford, last summer, Mr. Huxley points out that cosmic evolution and moral evolution are not only not identical or parallel, but are deadly contradictories. Men's moral victory means the suppression, the annulment, even, of certain terrible forces of the cosmic or natural kind.

But Spencer's panacea, or something as nearly as possible like it, has been tried, with results that whosoever will may study at his leisure. The French Revolution was based upon his thought of social advance. That movement and the English liberalism springing from it, had for their guiding principle the reduction to its lowest possible terms of all social interference with individual action and development. We now have little idea of the rapturous anticipations which liberal philanthropists then cherished in consequence of the great change. Edmund Burke presents some of these in his "Reflections upon the French Revolution." "What an eventful period is this!" exclaimed Dr. Price in a sermon, part of which Burke quotes, "I am thankful that I have lived to see it. I could almost say, 'Lord, now lettest Thou Thy servant depart in peace, for mine eyes have seen Thy salvation.'"

But the hopes of political liberals a century ago have not been fulfilled. Poverty has not come to an end. Injustice is still with us. Though wealth and culture have immensely advanced, it would be hard to disprove the assertion that the last hundred years, the age which liberalism justly and proudly calls its own, have been, in spite of so great progress, among the unhappiest on record. The poor are still here, wretched as ever, while those to whom have fallen the great nominal fortunes which the age has produced, find them ashes instead of gold. This century of liberalism is precisely the one in which pessimism has been born — pessimism, that is no longer the smart hobby of the few but the fixed conviction of multitudes. The course of the world, economically viewed, seems to belie all our notions of right and wrong. Trying to look upon men as brothers, we see them sundered into widely disparate and hostile classes by the operation of relentless law. The very theory of their brotherhood many now throw aside as an old wives' fable.

Suppose it admitted that social readjustments of one sort and another may more or less improve what is amiss in men's life together, the considerations adduced make it clear that nothing short of a moral betterment in men can change these evils radically. Another line of thought, I judge, makes this conclusion a real demonstration. It is a sadly convincing induction that when material advancement does chance to come to the poorer classes, as through a rise of wages or the cheapening of bread, the gain is instantly checked by an increase in population.

It is the custom to make light of Malthus. More or less thoughtful people are, in their own conceits, continually refuting him. Prince Krapotkin attempts this by showing from examples and by the principles of chemistry the indefinite improvableness in the fertility of land. Henry George smites Malthus by alleging that food is not acquired through agriculture alone, and that non-vegetable food, in the form of flesh and fish, may be multiplied almost without limit. Professor Atwater delivers his blow at Malthus by reciting the virtues of numerous food articles now thrown away. Other agricultural chemists attack Malthus by hinting at the possibility, indicated by some experiments, of developing various forms of plant life from the free nitrogen in the air, of which the supply is supposed to be practically unlimited, feeding pigs with the product and feeding men with the pigs. Still other anti-Malthusians try to make a point by remarking that though food-getting becomes harder and harder as years pass, the creation of other things needful to life, manufactured articles, including articles which minister to our higher wants, is to be easier and easier. Suppose bread-winning to become a hundred times as difficult as now, if manufacturing grows easier in the same degree, humanity will get its whole living with no greater exertion than now.

None of these suggestions is without interest or weight, yet all of them are relatively superficial, not in the least affecting the bed-rock truth which Malthus unearthed. Many as were Malthus's errors in expounding his law, slight and local as is the threat at present offered by the operation of that law, a Malthusian law exists, which cannot be set aside, over which it were far more seemly to look sober than to smile. Population tends to increase more rapidly than the means of subsistence; mouths multiply faster than meals. Of course, population cannot actually run beyond its food supply, but it incessantly tends to do so. What prevents the existence of absolutely foodless mouths, what keeps down men's numbers, is certain checks, partly preventive, partly repressive; the preventive ones including all causes which veto the origination of human life when it would otherwise originate; the positive, of whatever kills off our species, viz., wars, famines, vices, pestilences, and ordinary disease. A single reflection shows how active these checks have been in the past.

The present population of Europe could, by increasing at a rate no more rapid than that of its present growth, have sprung from a mere half million souls living in the year 400 A.D. But Wietersheim carefully estimates that long before 400, viz., during the second century, A.D., the European parts of the Roman Empire alone, to say naught of North Germany and Scandinavia, contained forty-five million souls. That is, Europe contained by 400 A.D. more than a hundred times people enough to have produced Europe's present population, supposing this to have increased at the same rate that now prevails. And, had Europe's actual population in the second century grown ever since then at the rate marked in the nineteenth, as it could not but have done had no checks been in play, Europe's present population would be 15,000,000,000 instead of 356,000,000.

Could the present growth of population possibly continue, the failure of standing room would be but a matter of time. The entire globe measures about 600,000,000,000 square yards, or, allowing a yard as standing room for four persons, there is place for 2,400,000,000,000,000 persons. Now the population of England and Wales, which may be regarded as about normal for civilized lands, doubled between 1801 and 1851. At this rate population would in 100 years multiply itself by 4; in 200 by 16; in 1,000 by 1,000,000; and in 3,000 years by 1,000,000,000,000,000,000. So that even if we start with a single pair, the increase would in 3,000 years have become two quintillion human beings: viz., to every square yard 3,333⅓ persons instead of 4. Or, the earth would be covered with men in columns of 833⅓ each, standing on each other's heads. If they averaged five feet tall, each column would be 4,166⅔ feet high.

In all or nearly all large cities the poorer classes are at all times visibly under the Malthusian law. They have a birth rate and a death rate far beyond what is normal, while the number of deaths caused by inanition and vices and by diseases consequent upon these, makes it clear that Malthus's repressive checks are in operation. In any society not moral enough to exercise self-restraint, population inevitably so augments that the poorest have barely food enough to support life, their numbers being kept down to what they are mainly by sheer lack of nutrition. Lessening *per capita* plenty, operating directly or else through vices, induces bodily weaknesses to which enough succumb to let the others continue.

Few or none of those dying actually starve to death. The picture of great populations literally starved is what Malthusianism, quite illegitimately, seems to suggest to most, and since our slums present no spectacle of that kind, many conclude that Malthus was a simpleton. Downright starvation is rare even in famines. Of most cases of death in such, the immediate cause is disease, which disease, however, is produced by lack of nourishment.

It boots nothing to know that few die from the niggardliness of nature, in the strict sense, which is true if you take large areas, so as not to light on famine spots; because the maladjustments of society are, even in Malthus's own discussion, conceived as practically part of nature. Beyond question, the earth's present population is none too great to be amply supported, could it but be properly distributed and organized, and all classes of it be rendered industrious. But the problem becomes no whit less forbidding in that "every prospect pleases and only man is vile." Human stubbornness is a very serious thing, and may abide to complicate the difficulty in its final form, when at last the resources of the soil do prove inadequate.

Three hard facts confront us. One is that the earth's stock of substances capable of sustaining life is, after all, limited. Another is that many of these are passing hopelessly beyond man's reach. The third is that such utilizing of plant nutrition as is intrinsically possible must for ever increase in cost. Less and less fruitful soils must be brought into use, loam reclaimed from beneath the ocean, rocks pulverized, to make place for new land and to furnish the mechanical ingredients for artificial soil. And, at best, such soil cannot but be limited in amount, so expensive will be its manufacture. Krapotkin's cases can never be generalized, involving, as they do, the limitless carting of heavy stuffs from farms to towns and from towns to farms. This particular cause of decrease in agricultural returns will indeed weaken as population condenses, but cannot disappear, since people can never be scattered evenly over the land.

As I conclude, then, the much ridiculed old doctrine of Malthus is, for substance, true, that some men's reproductive propensity needs governance. It is not, like their love for the beautiful, an inclination which it is for the general interest that we should everywhere encourage, but an appetite, part of man's animal nature, always to be kept under law.

"So long as unlimited multiplication goes on, no social organization which has ever been devised, or is likely to be devised, no fiddle-faddling with the distribution of wealth, will deliver society from the tendency to be destroyed by the reproduction within itself, in its intensest form, of that struggle for existence the limitation of which is the object of society. And however shocking to the moral sense this eternal competition of man against man or of nation against nation may be; however revolting may be the accumulation of misery at the negative pole of society, in contrast with that of monstrous wealth at the positive pole, this state of things must abide, and grow continually worse, so long as Istar holds her way unchecked. It is the true riddle of the Sphinx; and every nation which does not solve it will sooner or later be devoured by the monster itself has generated."*

---

* Huxley. *Nineteenth Century*, Feb., 1888, p. 669.

This, now, must not be misunderstood. There is nothing in Malthusianism, or in any facts of life, to render appropriate a crusade in favor of universal celibacy. Though parenthood which can lead only to immorality, misery, and lingering death should be discouraged, yet to the able, healthy, intelligent, well-to-do, especially to such as can instruct and lead their fellow-men, and can reasonably hope for offspring like themselves in this, parenthood may even be a duty.

The ideal earthly society would of course be one in which human beings were numerous enough to work the great cosmic field to the very best advantage, yet voluntarily few enough, and also just enough to each other, to admit of a reasonable and decent subsistence for all. To introduce such a state of things men must limit the work of Malthus's positive or repressive checks upon population, of those causes, that is, which diminish life after it has come into being, and impose the business of equating population and subsistence more and more upon the preventive checks of the moral sort. Let the energy which keeps down the census be preventive rather than repressive, and at the same time morally preventive, not immorally so.

Gentlemen, there is but one force capable of bringing about this benign result, this result so imperative if humanity is to advance. That force is character. Let the masses remain ignorant and brutal, and human life will for ever continue in threatening disproportion to food, wealth and poverty side by side, the comfort of a few shadowed by wars and want and sicknesses on the part of multitudes.. For man's body as for his soul, for time as for eternity, his only hope lies in spiritual elevation. The problem of human progress is the problem of improving human character.

As we are less sure than we would like to be touching the possibility of bringing about the moral reform necessary to social reform, it is proper, however painful, to think what is in store supposing the several ills now afflicting us to continue. A fate so bad as that may await us. The outlook for progress is in various ways most discouraging. At some points our course is retrograde. Social and private sins, as contrasted with crimes of violence, are undoubtedly on the increase. Thinking of the human race, its vices and its tendencies in our time, the sage queries to himself oftener than he likes to say it aloud:

>"Is the great flock
>For the good Balder, or the evil Lok?"

In numerous of its worst phases our age exactly resembles that which preceded the breaking up of the old Roman Empire. Many thoughtful persons are at this moment in terror of some signal social paroxysm like that. And it may come. God may please again, as he has so often done hitherto, to purify the air by a cyclone, or to heave up continents of rich loam by an earthquake.

If progress does not come, retrogression will come. Our woes will grow worse and worse, till there is a catastrophe. Society may go back to barbarism, and again have slowly to pull up the long hill which it has ascended since Western Rome fell before barbarian attacks.

One thing is sure: should the rankling hostilities of our lower classes to the aristocracy result in outright war, the upper forces of society will not conquer so easily as in former social wars. The common people are too well educated. Poor as their organization is, it is far better than they have ever had before. They might conquer, in which case there would be danger that many of the most precious results of civilization would again go by the board.

Among the philanthropists who admit that moral progress must condition general social progress, two different policies, neither of which, however, is meant wholly to exclude the other, are urged to secure the needed moral uplift. One is the usual policy of Christians, the use of exhortation and preaching, appeals to men's consciences and reason, little being expected from social changes or from any modification in men's mere outward estate. Devotees of this method in morals call attention to the fact that while desperate poverty and oppression are indeed foes to morality, yet men's moral elevation in general is not high or low in any exact proportion to their political or economic well-being.

This humble way of doing good is remarkably successful, much more so than one at first imagines. The Church is incessantly victorious. Her success in inspiring to a nobler life the layers of mortals accessible to her is astounding. The trouble is that while she is at work saving one relay of our fellows, the fatal profligacy of the vicious classes has brought in another relay more difficult to reach. We succeed only to find our unfinished task greater than when we began. Preaching is indispensable, yet some form of practice needs to co-operate. What is to moralize that vicious submerged tenth of society?

This question brings the socialist to his feet. Simply give people a chance to be well-off temporally, he says, and vices will vanish. Slums moral will disappear with slums economic. Marx taught that character is wholly the product of material conditions. Render the body comfortable and the soul will take care of itself. Social reform is not to await moral reform. The very reverse is the order.

I cheerfully grant that, though not alone or finally sufficient, the material elevation and encouragement of the masses would be a very valuable aid toward their moral amelioration. Yet, touching this, four observations are in place.

 1. How is the needed material improvement to begin? Where is the ποῦ στῶ for it? A moral ποῦ στῶ from which to begin is confessedly hard enough to find. Yet the search for such seems to me not quite so vain as that for the other.

 2. Different men's degrees of moral advancement do not parallel at all closely their relative ranks in material regards.

 3. In the last lecture, by adverting to the thriftless class in rural New England, where no aristocracy ever

ground the faces of the poor, where destitution has never been forced upon any, and where all social influences continually favor ambition and saving, it was shown that poverty and indolence are not always caused by forbidding material conditions.

4. The rich need moral improvement no less than the poor, and it does not appear how a system of socialism would effect this result. Will the proud millionaire, the bloated bondholder, the autocratic capitalist, feel more kindly towards his fellowmen after he has been obliged to share his fortune with them?

Nothing else seems to me to offer the hope of getting lower humanity triumphantly over the bar into the safe waters of progress, that might be afforded by the common school system if rightly developed and used.

What is needed is to raise the standard of living among the lowliest, to imbue the poorest people with such a sense of the dignity of life as to make them unwilling that children of theirs shall be doomed by poverty to live like brutes or like slaves, as so many now do.

That the standard of life is so low is the reason why such grinding poverty exists. Within large limits the laboring population can have in the way of reward for its exertions whatever it unitedly demands. The trouble is that so many are willing to work for starvation wages. These act as scab help and, by their competition, force down wages.

Could we create a universal sentiment throughout the labor community that a laborer ought to have about so much in order to make his life worth living, and could we render this sentiment so strong that it would be a check upon population, at the same time that it pressed from capital into laborers' hands all that ought to go as wages, dire poverty would disappear. Could we thus raise the standard of life sufficiently high, all poverty deserving the name would be gone forever.

Mr. Mill, in a famous chapter, has made it, I think, as good as certain that this vital operation of landing the lower orders of men high and dry upon the proper level of living, with an unwillingness to descend again or to allow their children to descend, cannot be carried through except in some more or less artificial manner. The public school system may be made a splendid instrument for the accomplishment of this needed result, elevating the standard of life among the masses of the people.

Let us have, first, compulsory education nine months of every year for every child till the age of fourteen. Let us also make the kindergarten part of the public school system, keeping up its natural and humanizing methods so far as possible in all the subsequent school years. Let us perfect the purely intellectual side of our schooling, securing the best teachers and the best appurtenances from the lowest up to the highest forms. We must also insist that in morality and culture, as well as in all æsthetic regards, every teacher shall be a perfect specimen of manhood or of womanhood.

In the next place, we must make every schoolhouse a

veritable palace, perfect in ventilation, light, warmth, and spaciousness, so that every moment of school time will be to the pupils one of physical delight. The architecture, external and internal, of schoolhouses must be the choicest and most approved. Flowers are to surround the building on every side in summer, and fill every niche inside in winter. Paintings, statuary, and other forms of art are to adorn every panel and corner, every stairway and corridor from top to foundation.

Twelve years of school life like this on the part of every member of our population would in a few generations change the national conception of what it is to live. It would multiply intelligence and morality, rendering the toilers determined and able to stand together for all their just rights. Moreover, population would be voluntarily limited so as to allow a decent plenty for all when all just rights now efficiently insisted on were granted. All this might be expected to come to pass also without any clash between social classes. No social cataclysm need occur, no new principle of sociology need be introduced. Wealth would not suffer, but, on the contrary, be immensely increased, since the ignorant work-population, ever the least productive economically, would be no more.

The realization of such a scheme nothing hinders but men's widespread apathy and unbelief. Even the dislike to the common school felt by a part of the Roman Catholic clergymen, could, I believe, be overcome were the possibilities of the plan properly exhibited. Some, I suppose, would say that our schools are not good enough to be applied to any such high or spiritual purpose. True, they are not at present good enough, but if all would join hands to make them the best they could possibly be, all that has been suggested might easily be wrought by their means.

Gentlemen, I am sure that this lecture must seem to you very unsatisfactory. It has shown how terrible is the problem of a worthy life for man here in this earth. It has, perhaps I may say, pointed a way to or toward the solution of that problem; but it has not solved it. In the present condition of moral and social science, it would be rash to presume to do more than to indicate the direction of hope. I unhesitatingly believe in a perfected humanity, but how, in precise or minute details, the perfection is to be wrought out, none can now say.

Permit me, in closing, to present, as voicing perfectly my thought, a poem written by my friend, William Shields Liscomb, who was laid in his grave but a few months ago, prematurely worn out by hard labor for and among the people of a foreign land.

THE OVERVOICE

I

Ofttimes unto my troubled heart it seems,—
Brooding the sin and sorrow of this age,
Its lust of gold, its hate, its hunger-rage,
Its clash of warring creeds, its torturing dreams,
Its love of man forgot in sordid schemes —
That earth has lost her spirit's heritage,
Like Esau's, trafficked for a paltry wage
Which the clear-flighted soul but mockery deems:
Till all the love I bore it grows estranged
Through loathing of this spirit that denies,
And even the world I gloried in seems changed
From music-throbbing earth and orblit skies
To that dim realm wherein great Dante ranged,
The eternal air all tremulous with sighs.

II

I heard by night a mighty voice that shrilled
Athwart the unmeasured spaces of the stars,
At sound whereof the world's rude strife and jars
To silence like eternity's seemed stilled: —
His voice with whose quick life all nature thrilled
Deeper than sorrow that corrodes the scars,
Deeper than hate that blights or sin that mars,
Pledging that earth's long hope should be fulfilled:
"From sluggish nebula to flaming sun,
From flaming sun to blossom-gendering sod,
Cycles of unimagined years have run —
Millions of æons but to form a clod.
Hast thou considered, then, how vast the span
Required to form at length the perfect man."

www.ingramcontent.com/pod-product-compliance
Lightning Source LLC
Chambersburg PA
CBHW031334160426
43196CB00007B/679